LEADERSHIP EXCELLENCE BY DESIGN

STRATEGIES FOR SUSTAINABILITY AND STRENGTH

Do great things!

Dr. Whela

ISBN-13:978-0692047156
ISBN- 10:0692047158

For I know the plans I have for you, declares the Lord, plans to prosper you and not harm you, plans to give you hope and a future.

Jeremiah 29:11

Dedication

To my husband Paul.
Thank you for supporting the leader in me.

To my daughter Amy and son, Kevin.
Thank you for being part of my "purpose."

To my tenderhearted son Joseph,
and father, Robert who are among the angels,
I miss you.

To my mother, Mary Ann, my first example of a strong, courageous leader.

To the little ones who light up my world,
grandsons, Grey J., Elon, and Wells.

Contents of Excellence

Introduction

Strong Leaders & Sustainable Organizations

Your organization, no matter how big or small, public or private, start-up or established, is a living, breathing body of people. Your people are filled with untapped potential waiting to be recognized and set into action. Your human talent is fundamental to your organizational endeavors. Their importance is demonstrated in both failure and success.

Leading your people takes being fully present, continuously influencing others toward a shared vision, and having the courage to mobilize your people for a successful outcome. Being a strategic leader is about having a broader vision – being ahead of the curve and thinking outside the box. Strategic leadership is also about having a well-planned roadmap to get you where you want to go.

Leadership is a partnership. Strategic leaders do not journey alone. They understand their mission and vision is advanced when they develop internal and external partnerships and become a *leader of leaders*.

Are you a strategic leader who aims to link people to process, organizational objectives to individual development, and success to sustainability? If not, now is the time to consider how your leadership may be hindering the progress of your organization.

Excellence by design is a daily act of knowing, being, and doing. Leading with excellence is a way of life. Excellence is a leadership style that embraces a call to go above and beyond.

Excellence requires leaders to be more than adequate, give more than take, and be at peace as they let go of power and control. By letting go, leaders make room to empower, build, and transform their workplace.

Regardless of your age, race, gender, title, or religious affiliation, the content of this book will posture your leadership toward designing for excellence. When leaders design strategic initiatives around the practices of excellence, a competitive advantage is realized.

Leadership development and professionalism are at the heart of excellence. Developing and executing people strategies contribute to accelerating the leadership pipeline. People strategies require intentional development activities that grow and bring your people into the leadership fold. When the development design is intentional, the outcome is high-performance contributors that create a powerful impact.

This book is for leaders who seek to raise their personal and organizational bar of leadership and build for strength and sustainability. This book is not a tool just for senior leaders. This book is for all who seek to rise and call themselves leader, regardless of title, gender, or length of service to your industry.

As you dive into the pages of this book, you will uncover age-old, historical principles that are relevant to 21st-century organizations. Each chapter tackles real-world conditions leaders face and encourages discussion of best practice leadership application to move the dial on today's organizations toward a better tomorrow. Moving the dial can be achieved through personal and professional excellence.

This book is written through the eyes of an organizational consultant, Gallup® Certified Strengths Coach, and a passionate researcher of both corporate and faith-based leadership practices.

At the end of each chapter, I seek to engage you in profound thought and reflection. Perhaps, to encourage and even change the way you see your role as a leader and the human talent who make up your organization. When the principles and practices of excellence are applied, a healthy, engaged culture emerges.

Enjoy the journey!

Dr. K. Whelan

Chapter 1

Leading Through Time

"When the leader gets better, everyone gets better."
~Craig Groeschel

The first scholarly book on leadership I read was *Leadership Theory and Practice*[1] authored by Peter G. Northouse, Ph.D., during my Master of Science in Administration program at Central Michigan University. A year later, I experienced great excitement when this same book was included on the reading list for a doctoral class at Regent University. My first thought, "one less book to buy and read," was quickly met with realism. The "learner" in me would whole-heartedly embrace the opportunity to turn the pages of this leadership text once again.

Re-reading the highlighted sections and notes in the margins gave me hope of gaining a better understanding of the crux of leadership. My goal was to understand because the more I read on the topic of leadership, the more I found leadership shifted through ages, phases, and cultures. The definition of leadership never really seemed to land on a firm foundation. Each writer proudly presented their ideas and interpretation, each theorist their position. The word leadership did not have a standard definition.

As I considered this fact, I wasn't surprised. The role of a leader is based on diverse views that lead to different expectations on how leadership is delivered but also received. The role of national and organizational culture, gender, generation, and yes, religious views can create conflict, inaction, and uncertainty for leaders and their organization. Leading people into the leadership fold requires continuous improvement practices that begin with you, the leader.

When I think of my leadership journey, I realize it is a journey of many factors. Yes, I read a lot of books and research in the field of leadership. I welcome opportunities to learn and develop my leadership, and I couple my learning with instinct. However, I believe even more importantly, I learned to model my leadership after the strong, confident, encouraging women and men in my life whose talents have been put to work across the diverse industries they serve. Interestingly, many of these leaders invite faith-based principles into their leadership as a way to maintain their personal and professional standards of excellence.

Too often, leadership practices are mimicked by character that has missed the excellence mark. As leaders, we must have the courage to act rightly and provide a model of leadership to be emulated.

Pause here. Reach back into your memory and ask yourself:

Who is or has been your leadership role model?

What is it about this leader that left an imprint?

Was it their style, attitude, their ability to demonstrate what you define as great leadership? Or, perhaps, they were an example not to emulate, having a narcissistic, controlling, micro-managing, or power-hungry leadership style?

What is the "feeling" you get when you bring this leader to mind? Be specific.

How has this leader positively or negatively influenced your leadership? Be specific.

Whether this leader brings about fond memories or memories you would rather forget, did you ever have a conversation around the positive or negative impact their leadership had on you?

Leadership is a continuous journey. I may have asked who has been your leadership role model and why, but more importantly, you must ask yourself the question: What does my leadership convey to others? Is it effective? Am I leading through a lens of excellence?

When it comes to feedback, the good, the bad, and the ugly helps a leader understand their leadership style and the positive or negative influence their leadership has on others. When done right, offering and being accepting of feedback encourages a culture of honest communication, builds trust, increases intimacy, and positions leadership forward.

Picking Leadership Apart To Put It Back Together

If you take yourself back to elementary school, you learned a noun is a person, place, or thing. According to the Merriam-Webster dictionary, the words leader and leadership are both nouns. If you lead by position, I would argue your leadership rests here, but it can't stay there! Your leadership must be an activity. If you lead by direction, actively engaging your people, your leadership is in an actionable state. If "x" marks the leadership spot, this is where you want to be, actively leading.

To supplement the development of the word leadership and continue to illuminate its ambiguity, Dr. Bruce Winston and Dr. Kathleen Patterson developed an integrative definition of leadership by addressing the elements of leadership in detail. The research duo entertained over 150 articles and books that contained a definition, scale or construct of leadership and characterized them into 91 leadership dimensions.[2] Yes, 91! You, as a leader, are more than a title and more than a one-sentence definition.

Winston and Patterson's definition promotes an aggressive way forward as it unveils numerous identifiable leadership characteristics, skills, and behaviors to ponder and assess. Their interpretation captures differing views of leadership and pushes the leadership definition forward with modern-day eyes.

As leaders, we are asked to reach in and discover what true leadership encompasses. Current research supports the notion that leaders are not, and maybe, more importantly, cannot be one-dimensional. Uncovering 91 dimensions of leadership means leaders and leadership are multi-faceted. Therefore, leaders must promote ongoing learning and development to support and enhance their presence, vision, and positioning of their organization and the people they serve.

Like the once limited definition of leadership, the practice of leadership must continue to be poked and prodded. Leadership has changed in meaning as scholars, researchers, and scientists have been able to define science behind the theory. As research continues to question and push the leadership envelope, and as innovation and creativity align with foresight and future, additional leadership definitions and methodology continue to emerge.

New theories and new interpretations, such as those provided by Winston and Patterson, mean that the rules are changing, and change can constitute a revolutionary impact on leadership. The refinements of leadership theory project a broader, more in-depth look at the requirements, processes, and behaviors of a leader, generating a multi-dimensional platform for our consideration.

As we move from analytic thinking about the definition of leadership to systems thinking, we find interconnectedness amongst varying parts. Science proclaims theory and fact must find agreement. This author argues the Winston and Patterson integrative definition of leadership does just this. They make the case that the role and actions of leadership must be congruent.

Science seeks to find truth. Therefore, those working to refine leadership theory must observe and integrate the building blocks that are necessary to end in truth. For many leaders, including me, the building blocks of truth rest in research, but also in the Word of God.

The Mantle of Leadership

Leadership is one of those things that you are either born into, fall into, are commanded into, or are chosen as leader. Members of the Royal family of England are born into a leadership role. Mega-church Pastor Joel Osteen fell into leadership when he reluctantly took the pulpit after his father passed away. In the Bible, Moses received the role of leader through a direct commandment from God. What about you? Perhaps you were chosen to fill the role of leader?

Whether born, fell, commanded or chosen, being a leader does not mean you are equipped and ready for the role. Conversely, being a leader does not mean that you will fail because of how you received the position. Even if you're not ready, don't feel worthy, or are downright scared of being in charge, there is good news! Although it may come or even look easy for some, leadership is something that must continually be developed regardless of the level of leadership you provide.

The activities required for the role of leadership, followership, relational partners, and contributors in and outside the workplace remain a choice. This choice is regardless of how you've come to leadership or the knowledge, skills, or innate traits you have or have not acquired.

Got Traits?

Historically and collectively, many theorists argued leaders were born and exhibited innate qualities that separated them from the average member of the group. Character, whether upright or corrupt, was identified. Although the term "leadership" has existed for centuries, it is the Great Man and Trait Theory of the 20th-century that were the first attempts to study leadership. These early theories speculate a leader's effectiveness rather than provide validation.

If you have attended one of my speaking engagements on leadership, there is a good chance you have witnessed the trait theory in action. I often bring this theory in to create an impression for the audience. This impression generates an image of how leadership has changed over time.

What researchers have come to know is leadership is more than being born a great leader with enhanced traits that create successful organizations. Instead, leadership is made great in the collectiveness of the body, which makes up the organization. Leadership qualities and traits alone do not make a for an effective leader. If 21st-century organizations continue to look at leadership through the *traits only-Type A personality lens*, organizations are missing crucial leadership opportunities that foster diversity, innovation, and sustainability.

Science has played a significant role in advancing leadership theory. The science of any kind is about seeking to further and expand areas that are not explained by current theory. In keeping with this thinking and approach, a theory is about progression and changing direction, keeping things fresh based on new findings and innovative thinking. The old way of leading based on early science and theory is continuously in the state of change.

Thomas Kuhn, the author of *The Structure of Scientific Revolutions*, warns against forcing nature into boxes.[3] The Great Man and Trait Theory is one of those boxes. As is, these early leadership models are outdated and no longer relevant based on the contribution of science that validates leadership is more than early theorists acknowledged. If society relied on the trait theory alone, we would have tall, charismatic, male-extroverts leading our organizations. Instead, we have come to understand leadership is for all, not just a select few. Why? Because everyone has influence. Our influence is found internally as we lead our organizations and externally through our networks.

Research provides us with the theory that leadership evolution and organizations of today are not the top-down functioning organizations of yesterday, but are comprised of networks, clusters, and ad-hoc task forces.

Think about your networks. How have they changed? Leading and communicating via the world wide web has expanded our networks as well as opportunities to influence.

In the 21st-century, networks, clusters, and ad-hoc task forces look like LinkedIn, Facebook, and YouTube. The conventional Business After Five Chamber of Commerce events have expanded to everyday individuals creating local meet-ups. These leaders reach beyond their local networks, streaming live events that span across the globe.

Relationship marketing and building networks have taken on a whole new meaning with the advancement of technology. The information superhighway has made global networking, team-building, and operations possible with the click of a button. Advances in communication, education, and strategy make it possible to lead and serve right where you are regardless of location.

It's Not My Job

There is reciprocity that is necessary when designing for excellence no matter what generation you were born. It is at this juncture where leaders, followers, and contributors connect, unite, and collectively sustain the organization through service. However, service in and of itself is a characteristic that some leaders stumble over. Maybe you're thinking, "It's not my job to serve. It's my job to lead."

How are *you* demonstrating excellence through service?

In a former position as Executive Director, I made it clear to every person I interviewed that I would never ask them to do something I haven't already done. If it was 5 pm and I wasn't in my office, there was a pretty good chance you would find me in the kitchen doing the dishes. Why? Because it wasn't beneath me to do so.

Doing the dishes in this instance is not a metaphor, but I'm asking you to remember it as one. Are you allowing your worldly title to get in the way of doing the dishes?

What some may see as a lowly act of service is an example of tremendous influence. Influence through service creates impact. This type of influential impact is a principle of leadership excellence. We must learn to embrace our inner influence and *step in* to serve right where we are regardless of title.

Your organizational title or level on the alphabet soup senior leader hierarchy chart does not have to begin with the letter "C" (Chairman, Chief), "D" (Director), "E" (Executive), "P" (President) (Pastor), or "V" (Vice President) to lead, serve, and create impact.

Sure, we lead our organizations, but we also lead our committees, volunteer teams, our families. And, don't forget you lead yourself! Therefore, leadership and serving others, regardless of title, must be executed at every level of the organization.

Championing Leadership

When you think leadership, never discount the contribution you make regardless of what title you hold. Today's organizations need a champion, someone to step up, lead with purpose, and intentionally pave the way for others.

Organizations cannot function without people. They are and will forever be the key to organizational success.

Getting everyone looking in the same direction takes work. While that work begins with senior leaders, it can't stay there. There must be a continued push to bring leaders into the fold by ditching a leadership of one mentality and instead generate a *leader of leaders* culture that spans both broad and deep.

In each of the following examples, an employee demonstrated leadership, and none were in the elite C-suite.

"Paul took charge and saved lives in Afghanistan." (Physician Assistant)

"The event was a success because Marie helped non-profit donors envision the outcome of their giving." (Development Coordinator)

"Patsy went the extra mile, following up to be sure the guests were happy with their accommodations." (Hotel Front Desk Associate)

"Michael built relationships and demonstrated what it looks like to take care of his customers." (Customer Service Representative)

Influence is found at all levels of the organization. However, it often goes unnoticed or undetected. It's up to leaders to shift their mindset from being a "leader" to becoming a leader of leaders. A leader of leaders helps others be the hero of their leadership story. As leaders serve their people, their people will be empowered to lead.

Would you be surprised to learn that when asked, about 80% of your people will self-select out of leadership? It's true. It's up to you as a leader to give your people permission to lead! To demonstrate excellence and create sustainability, leadership must be the expectation. When leadership authority is confidently delegated and supported over time, organizations build for sustainability and strength.

The Coaching Corner

1. What is your definition of leadership?
2. How does your definition of leadership align with your actions?
3. If I asked, "Are you a leader?" before reading this chapter what would your response be?
4. How has your answer changed after reading this chapter? Why?
5. Describe how you received your current leadership role (born into, commanded into, chosen into, or fallen into).
6. How has the "how" you acquired your position impacted your role as a leader?
7. What does service look like to you and, how are you demonstrating this in and out of the workplace?

Chapter 2

Foundational Leadership

"Vision with action can change the world."
~Joel A. Barker

Leadership is relational and intentional. Leadership is multi-faceted. You may hear some leaders say, "you can't drift into great leadership." My humble opinion is, you can. You can drift into great leadership as easy as you can drift out of great leadership. Executing the mantle of leadership with distinction is a continuous process of learning and practicing excellence. Leadership and the practice of excellence is a choice.

Regardless of how you have come to leadership, three foundational practices separate a good leader from a great leader: presence, vision casting, and positioning. As simple as this may sound, today's leaders are failing as they neglect the importance of these three fundamental principles of leadership.

If a leader is not showing up (presence), casting and influencing others toward a meaningful goal (vision), and mobilizing their people into the leadership fold (positioning), leaders will not create or generate positive impact and sustainability for their organization.

Presence   Vision   Position

The Practice of Presence

When a leader is engaged, presence is communicated. Showing up is more than a warm body in a chair. Presence is not passive. Presence takes time and energy. Presence is showing up, actively participating in verbal communication with your leaders, team members, and external partners.

> *Presence is the opposite of absence.*

Leadership presence dares to have an open-door policy, perhaps even stepping outside the office, willing to embrace the vulnerability this may bring. A leader with presence asks questions like, "How can I best serve you?" "What's on your mind?" Sometimes presence is silence, showing up with a listening ear.

In my field of work, presence is not an option. It's crucial to make my presence count. When I am asked to consult, coach an individual, team, or speak to a group, I am not just physically present; I am psychologically present. If presence is the opposite of absence, which are you?

Maybe you don't have an office. Perhaps you work virtually. This is even more of a reason to active your presence. In my practice, 80% of the work I perform is completed by phone or video conference. I have to be actively present in each moment regardless of the communication method. Many of my clients cannot visually "see" me, but they are surely able to tell if I'm not demonstrating presence.

Presence is relational and must be practiced inside and outside the workplace. Regardless of time or virtual space that is between your internal *and* external partners, presence is required.

Here are some questions to consider:

1. How do you engage with the people in your organization?
2. How do you engage with your virtual or external partners?
3. How do you demonstrate active listening? (Concentrating on the conversation, responding appropriately, and remembering what is said.)
4. Who do you work with? What are their names? What's important to them?
5. Are you approachable? How do you know? Have you asked anyone?

Rate your leadership presence on a scale of 1 [low] to10 [high]. Where do you fall? If you find yourself on the low side of presence, there is good news! Presence is a skill. Because presence is a skill, when practiced, presence is strengthened.

Presence matters. Spending time developing leadership presence makes the difference between success and failure for a leader, and collectively for your organization.

The Power of Visioning

If you are leading and have no purposeful direction, you're not going to get very far. If you already have leadership presence, there's a good chance you effectively cast vision. Or, do you?

Vision is your preferred future; it's strategic, comprises the macro level, and lets others know where you are headed. So, do you know where you are headed? Be honest.

In 2007, I drove from upstate NY to San Antonio, Texas. I knew my endpoint but needed to rely on an old-fashioned paper map and signposts to get me to my destination. If I had a compass, I might have been able to go in the right direction for a while, but to get to my exact location would take a bit more effort.

When was the last time you drove to a new destination without a map app? A clear destination and direction are similar to your vision. No vision equals no direction. No direction means you are driving without purpose. If you are driving your organization without purpose, you are leading in the dark.

Leaders set the course for everyone they serve. If you have not created and shared your vision with your people, you must start today.

Vision casting is not a once and done activity. A leader's vision is meant to stay fresh and at the forefront of the minds of internal and external partners. It's your responsibility as a leader to influence toward a *shared* vision.

For leaders whose strength is deep strategic thinking, it's important to remember, if you've crafted a vision, that vision can't stay ruminating in your head. A vision must be shared with all levels of the

> *As a leader, it's your responsibility to influence toward a shared vision.*

organization to increase the likelihood of success. If everyone is not looking in the same direction, the leader has not done his or her job casting the vision.

Have you ever wondered why some or maybe no one is following or connecting with your vision? Perhaps you haven't painted your people *into* the picture. Your vision should be why people are excited to come to work. Is it?

Today's organizations are a melting pot of national cultures, genders, generations, and religious affiliations. Within those walls, the leader is responsible for creating the vision for the company with the intent to have everyone looking in the same direction. If no one knows or *understands* that direction, how can the organization, leader, or employee be successful? Without a concrete notion of leadership coupled with a robust, meaningful vision consistently pushed down and throughout the company, failure is imminent. If your people have no direction, how can you terminate their employment because they had a poor performance review?

Too many times, leaders are not keeping the vision alive. If you want to take a quick pulse check, get out of your chair and ask the next five people you see or talk to:

1. What is the leader's vision?

2. How does your individual role in the organization

    contribute to the leader's vision?

Better yet, do a "walk-around" in your workplace and get input at all levels of the organization. Don't be surprised by what you find. Sadly, most of your employees have no clue; they're showing up to work and collecting a paycheck instead of realizing the incredible impact their *part* contributes to the *whole* organization. The responses you get should give you enough information to right any wrongs and quickly get everyone looking in the same direction.

What's your vision for your organization, your team, your committee, or even your family? Is everyone on the same page? If not, it's time to understand "what and who" [it's going to take] to bring your vision to fruition. Positioning the right people is key.

Purposefully Positioning Your People

Leading with excellence is a continuous dance between leaders and the people they serve. How are you getting your people positioned to act on the vision you cast? Leaders mobilize their organizations by having the right players on the team who will carry the thought, idea, or defined vision from point A to point B.

When you think about how you position and motivate others, what's working? Maybe more importantly, what's *not* working? Here's a tip. When you figure out what's not working, STOP doing what's not working! You'll save yourself time, energy [which often comes out in the form of frustration], financial and human resources. Do you have talent in your organization to champion? Research suggests you may be making some critical mistakes when it comes to keeping your employees and contributors.

> *Leading with excellence is a continuous dance between leaders and the people they serve.*

A trillion dollars a year is lost to voluntary turnovers.[4] Organizations are paying hand over fist in recruitment, hiring, training and productivity initiatives. Yet, your people are exiting the doors of your organization. More than half state their exits could have been prevented.

Creating a culture of leaders who are driven by the mission and vision of your organization, and realize the impact of their contribution will increase engagement and decrease your talent exiting the workplace.

We will talk more about purposeful positioning and building teams in a later chapter.

The Coaching Corner

1. In what ways has your leadership presence helped or hurt a professional or personal relationship, project, or the organizational culture?
2. What vision are you casting for your organization? Your team? Your committee? Your family?
3. Does your leadership vision provide a clear cognitive and emotional direction for others to understand and follow? How do you know?
4. Describe how you keep your vision alive, or how the leader of your organization keeps the vision alive.
5. How do the people under your leadership demonstrate they know their role?
6. What motivates your people to show up to work each day?
7. Why are people exiting your workplace? What's one action step toward preventing this?
8. When you think about your role in the organization, were you a purposefully positioned hire?

Chapter 3

The Entrepreneur Leader

"It's critical to have a community that can cheer for you, cry with you and share relevant experiences, contacts and ideas."
~Liz Bohannon

There you are at your favorite restaurant, and from the table in back of you, you hear the voice of a woman say, "I'm an entrepreneur." You think to yourself, "Boy, I'd like to say that someday," but begin to laugh, thinking, "how can I *be one* if I can't even spell or pronounce the word correctly!" Your ears perk up, anticipating what she might say next, but the conversation fades as the waiter asks for your order and drowns out the conversation.

Entrepreneurs are the poster child of determination and accomplishment. They challenge the unknown and seek opportunity, which often comes with an element of risk. There are as many niches as there are glitches in the world of business. Instead of complaining or leaving life's innovations up to chance, it's up to each of us to see how to improve upon what the current market provides. You may be thinking, "I'm just not creative enough to do that."

Do you believe you are creative? Interestingly, just like in the case of self-selecting out of leadership, most people self-select out of creativity.

Lean in…you *are* creative and have *permission* to explore and expand creativity because it is breathed into you. Your creativity is a form of worship[5] and our human life expression.[6] When we are creative, we mimic our Creator's creativity through the work of our minds and hands.[7] Therefore, any barriers that are within the organization that impede the creative process must be removed.[8] This includes your own thinking!

During the creative process, the mind must be open to interpreting what may seem odd, uncomfortable, or even confusing at the onset. Leaders must trek into unchartered territories in order to seize success by incorporating self-reflection, a critical skill to find blind spots and biases in thinking.[9]Through the creative process, we are challenged to apply and look for holes in our own personal thinking, and in our organizational problem-solving process.

The Lie

Too many people, perhaps even you, are stifling creativity and innovation. Either because you told yourself you aren't creative or someone else led you to believe so. Guess what? It's a lie! The idea of being creative comes down to giving yourself permission to explore and expand creativity. You, too, can be the next Kiran Mazumdar-Shaw, Founder of the Indian Bio-Pharmaceutical company Biocon, or Craig Groeschel, U.S. Pastor, church planter, and leader of an innovative team at Life.Church. These leaders and their innovations have dramatically changed their sectors because they chose to go where others have not.

Gary Oster, DSL reminds, "…few consumers requested an iPhone until Apple, Inc. produced one. Nonetheless, those inventions dramatically changed the world and redefined their industries."[10] Apple has led the way for creativity and innovation in the technology sector. Their fearless leader, the late Steve Jobs, and his team sought to do what others may have thought to be unthinkable; bring technological imagination to life. We must learn to embrace 'what can be' and 'what is not,' not just 'what is.'

Whether it's Walt Disney's pioneer of animation, Oprah Winfrey's entertainment empire, or Jeff Bezos innovative approach to online purchasing with Amazon, these well-known entrepreneurs began with an idea and a desire. Through creativity, innovation, and

You are creative and have permission to explore and expand creativity because it is breathed into you.

drive, they have made a difference to the people they serve both directly and indirectly.

Sure, these organizations may have had and still may have doubts on the direction of innovations, or what the outcome of a "big idea" might be. What sets these leaders apart is that they remain obedient to the call. They move forward even if their idea, design, or re-design seemed out in left field.

The good news is, these leaders are no different than you and me. Each have 24 hours in a day, have commitments outside of work, and have openly shared uncertainty and failure during their leadership. The difference that most people fail to talk about is the need to recognize that your voice, your idea, and your impact is important. Bringing thought to action regardless of if your innovation ends up being a failed attempt is necessary. Why? Because leaders who have created the most significant impact learned to fail forward.

Characteristics of the Entrepreneur Leader

What does an entrepreneur leader look like? Many may think this breed is a well-dressed, sophisticated, smart-talking leader. Although all or part of this may be correct, it is not always the case. The entrepreneurs I interviewed varied in age, education, industry, and background. Most of the entrepreneurs I spoke with learned on the fly. One exclaimed, "I've never even read a book on leadership!" Still, all agree, either they need to be, or someone on their team needs to be well-versed in the field they're in. What remained the same were the characteristics of what they felt an entrepreneur should display.

Research suggests entrepreneurial orientation consists of being proactive, confident, anticipates future demand, and not afraid of risk. According to my research, these are true. In addition, passion and perseverance are necessary to push entrepreneurs through the obstacles. And yes, there will be obstacles!

The obstacles entrepreneurs face are real. An entrepreneur should not be surprised if they're laughed at, people stop taking their calls, or they get the door slammed in their face. You'll be in good company. Let's face it, not everyone will like your idea, product, or service, and that's okay. If you are not willing to sacrifice or hear the word "no," entrepreneurship is not for you.

My research asked entrepreneurs what would be important to relay to someone thinking about becoming an entrepreneur. The benefit as several of the leaders relayed is a double-edged sword. They have the opportunity to relish in their successes, knowing they were the creator of something spectacular. Many shared their decision to innovate has afforded them financial freedom, respect, and a sense of "making it." However, they all face the reality of if they fail; the failure rests on their shoulders. Entrepreneurs must be willing to accept responsibility and accountability for everything they do. Not everyone is ready to take on that responsibility.

Entrepreneurship also offers the benefit of personal growth. The automotive President I spoke with relayed, "One sure thing about becoming an entrepreneur is, you'll find out a lot about yourself." Another said, "You'll see how far, how long, and at what cost are you willing to incur on the road to success. The truth is, at the end of the day, you need to look yourself in the mirror and be okay with who you see, have become, and the decisions you've made along the way. Not everyone can do that."

Do You Play Well With Others?

Creativity and innovation do not happen in a vacuum and takes more than one person to make the endeavor a success. There seems to be a consensus that holds true with the entrepreneurial journey. You don't, can't and shouldn't walk this road alone. You must create a network of forward-thinking people who help get you where you want to go. As one entrepreneur put it, you need "an army of specialist, all with requisite skills and education" to make things work.

Entrepreneurs have to be good communicators, be able to develop relationships, *and* play nicely in the sandbox even when things don't go their way. Having a team that embraces the same commitment as the Founder will prove to advance the vision of the leader and the success of the team. Without commitment, innovation and creativity, projects, and motivation stalls.

Trustworthiness and reciprocity are birthed out of our social networks, and it's not the size, but the impact of those individuals that's important. Communicating an environment of collaboration and collective behavior brings about a shared identity and an affirmed value to the team. When the entrepreneur leader surrounds her or himself with *all in* team members who know their role and stay in their lane of expertise, the project has an increased likelihood of being successful. This does not mean that they work in a vacuum. Team members are willing to learn how the other 'spokes on the wheel' work toward rolling out the leader's vision.

The entrepreneur leader needs a team who is open to learning and understanding more than one aspect of the business, especially in the initial phase of operations. If team members are not all in, ethnocentrism, corruption, and prejudice may appear. This must be minimized.

It's important to identify, and at times *weed-out* your team members who may do you more harm than good. It's also important to be confident. However, when vanity meets opportunity, it's not always a pretty picture. It's not uncommon for entrepreneurs to walk an unethical line to get where they need to go or are taken advantage of by people who prey on their blind spots.

Several of the Founders I spoke with revealed the difficulty and disappointment they experienced when people they trusted took advantage. Uncomfortable life-long lessons occur when this happens. We've seen it a hundred times as companies try to make the big bucks at others' expense only to end up shut down, imprisoned, or stripped of their dignity. The take-a-way…keep yourself and the team you're building in check.

Do You Have DRIVE?

Although *all* leaders need drive, the solo and entrepreneur leaders need to kick drive into *over-drive*! Without DRIVE, the mindset and innovations that could dramatically change the world are in jeopardy.

For the entrepreneur leader, uncertainty is never far away. Being dedicated to run the race with perseverance helps during these times. By demonstrating resiliency, the entrepreneur leader will not be consumed by potential innovative failed attempts. Instead, the entrepreneur has the determination to stay focused on what creates desired outcomes. Conversely, these leaders must also know 'when to say when.' Identifying the difference between short term pain and terminal failure is key.

DRIVE

- Dedicated
- Resilient
- Innovative
- Visionary
- Enthusiastic

Leaders understand without vision; there is no direction. Vision is crucial for an entrepreneur. Entrepreneurs need to be visionaries for their projects and envision their success. The entrepreneur leader must also be enthusiastic. Why? Because these leaders may find they are their biggest, and sometimes their only cheerleader.

The entrepreneur must surround themselves with others who will share in their excitement. These same people are your sounding board and truthful tongue when needed. Having a support system will help get the entrepreneur through difficult times.

The entrepreneur leaders I spoke with had an "entrepreneurial drive." Their earlier entrepreneurial ventures became the springboard to where they are today. For example, one leader started a beach volleyball league in the middle of upstate NY at 19 years old. He had no experience raising capital, speaking to the City Council, or marketing, yet, he was successful in his endeavors. This leader now spends his time raising millions of dollars for his biotech company.

Another entrepreneur leader began his first business venture at 22. This lasted less than a year, noting he didn't have "enough experience, financing, and the timing wasn't right." This leader's second business lasted three years before transitioning in 2007 to his current automotive business, where he is President.

I come from a lineage of solo and entrepreneurs. My maternal great-grandfather came to America and formed a successful family plumbing business. At the age of 12, my maternal grandfather arrived on Ellis Island with nothing more than hope and a dream. My grandfather's dream, to be a successful barber shop owner, became a reality and financially positioned him to be the first immigrant to build a home in the 'east end' of town. This was unheard of in the 1950s. My paternal grandfather served the people in our community as a dairy owner, and later the owner and operator of coin-operated laundromats. My youngest brother has experienced his share of the entrepreneurial drive over the years and isn't stopping anytime soon.

You don't have to come from a family of entrepreneurs to be one. Like anything else in life, it's a choice. A decision to commit, backed with preparation, drive, and actionable steps, will get you where you want to go.

Are You Prepared?

The entrepreneurs I spoke with were in agreement that you have to plan. In fact, one said, "plan, plan, plan, and have a backup plan with an exit strategy." The risk is real for the entrepreneur. This journey is not for everyone. The leaders agreed, if you're not ready to risk your finances, time, energy, and in some cases, have severed or fractured relationships, then entrepreneurship is not for you.

One respondent always knew he wanted to be an entrepreneur, he didn't know exactly when, what, or how this would happen, still, he prepared himself. He prepared himself by living frugally, for a time when he would be able to commit. His forethought proved to be invaluable. This executive ventured into a high-risk, high return endeavor. Because of his financial preparedness approach, he was able to leave his former employer ten years ago to work fulltime at positioning his company towards success. During our interview, he stated, "an entrepreneur doesn't have to be a gambler, but does need to be someone who can decide, evaluate, and accept risk."

The Executive Director of a nonprofit noted, "There are as many headaches as there are rewards. Be ready to put in a lot of work to get your business up and running. And, if you can't commit to coming in Monday morning even if you don't know if you're getting paid, you're not cut out for this." Struggling for capital is a theme that was evident in all my interviews. Amazingly, it hadn't stopped any of the leaders as of this writing.

Failure Is Not Fatal

Most people see the entrepreneur through starry eyes, making money hand over fist from their successful innovation. That may be true for some. The truth is, success does not happen overnight. Success often takes years, coupled with extraordinary challenges for a venture to meet with success. The biotech executive I spoke with tells me he and his partner had daily successes and failures in their start-up phase. The biggest success to date is that they have not experienced terminal failure. They made some relationship mistakes along the way, but continue to persevere.

The myth that those who create are masterful makers having triumphed in the straight line of success is a falsehood. It typically takes a lot of effort, hard work that includes muttering the "f" word more times than not. Yes, the word FAILURE.

Many years ago, I met an intelligent, Christian woman who became my mentor as I navigated the start-up phase of a multi-level marketing distributorship. I remember her telling me "never be afraid of the word 'no' because it's one step closer to a yes." She's been in business for over 30 years, and learned to accept failure and celebrate it! This statement alone provides the start-up entrepreneur with a new perspective on rejection.

It is through seemingly failed attempts or allowing for boundary-less possibilities, that creative behaviors are cultivated with putting thought into action, and repeating. Ask yourself, what would have happened if 3M never turned their "sticky" mistake into the Post-it Note? I know my life would not be the same, and neither would the shareholder's wallets without this practical, colorful concept that has become an office staple.

Leaders with an entrepreneurial spirit are not afraid to "do" things differently, or be paralyzed by the reality that failure is real. In times of uncertainty, the great leaders who push the envelope and themselves past FEAR are the ones who demonstrate grit. I imagine the entrepreneurs who are open and honest in sharing their journey would tell you that *giving up* remains an option that they may or may not struggle with. However, if you are a gritty leader, pushing through the disappointment and pain, the long hours, and the uncertainty, is part of the entrepreneur's reality. Learning how to react and reboot from failure will dictate the outcome.

Creating an environment where creativity flourishes begins with the leader establishing an organization that knows their direction, dissuades complacency, provides a physical environment conducive to creativity, and attracts recruits in support of innovation.[11]

Creating a culture of innovation takes courage and a leader who is visible and not afraid of failing forward.

When I look at my journey of solo and entrepreneurship, I think back to baking cheesecakes at the age of 21. I had no idea what I was doing! I knew I wanted [and needed] to earn money, had a desire to work for myself, and knew how to bake an exceptional cheesecake. *Knowing* this wasn't enough. My business plan and strategy for building a business were nonexistent. I quickly gave up my idea of creating a cheesecake empire. Why? Because I was leaving my success to chance. Chance is a sure strategy that will fast-track you and your big idea to a failed attempt.

My venture as an independent decorator followed my failed attempt to build that cheesecake empire. Again, I had no direction, and after a few years, I transitioned into becoming an independent distributor of wellness products. It was here where I learned some vital leadership and relationship marketing strategies. However, this, too, would end after a few years.

Regardless of holding for profit or nonprofit status, funding is a constant struggle for many entrepreneurs. My social entrepreneur endeavor as Founder of a nonprofit lasted until funding became close to nonexistent, and personal loss interrupted any would-be victories.

Deciding to close the doors in 2007 was difficult and not without many anxious days and sleepless nights. Unlike the other 'businesses' that I was unsuccessful in developing, this business was successful and held meaning.

The idea for the project was birthed out of serving. Giving back to the community where I was born and raised in a way that I knew how. My heart for business and children seemed like a match made in heaven. This, coupled with research suggesting that there was a need for a fresh, innovative, higher-end child development center, gave the project wings.

The nonprofit provided families a safe environment for their children. The business also afforded employment opportunities to men and women in the community, my teenage children, and a learning environment for early childhood students studying at the local community college.

The exit strategy was painful. After the public announcement, the doors closed fairly soon. Many of the families I served were left scurrying to find care. Within weeks, my staff was unemployed; I was unemployed, and everything I worked hard to provide was coming to an end. I felt like a failure.

Endings and feeling like a failure are hard. Endings and the 'f' word should never prevent the entrepreneur from dreaming, creating, or pushing themselves toward future strategies. The learning I experienced through this and earlier endeavors helped position me for what was to come.

Developing strong, courageous leaders is what I am called to do. My passion for helping others lead with confidence begins by unlocking the leader's authentic self. Perhaps this is due to my life long journey and love of self-improvement and development, or learning to press in and act confident even when I felt face down in the mud. Regardless of the reason, leadership development is my mission field.

My current role and what will [probably] be my entrepreneur finale as CEO of Belem Leaders and President of the nonprofit, Naples Leaders, has unknowingly been years in the making. Acknowledging through faith that there is always a greater plan for my life, allowed me to fail forward and rise from the ashes of derailment. I learned in pain; there is purpose. Because of both, I gained strength and found myself well-equipped to begin the entrepreneur journey again, this time more intelligently.

Some view failed attempts as a terminal failure or bad leadership. The entrepreneurs who get up from a kneeling position after a one-two-punch are survivors. Survivors are strong. Survivors are open to being vulnerable and accept failure as a lesson so they learn, grow, and continue toward the future they are called to create.

Theodore Roosevelt's *Citizen in a Republic* speech holds encouragement for the entrepreneur. The words acknowledge pain and suffering, but also great satisfaction in triumph and achievement. Even if the entrepreneur meets with failure, these leaders have gone where others have dared to go. This in and of itself is admirable.

A portion of Roosevelt's speech follows.

> "It is not the critic who counts; not the man who points out how the strong man stumbles, or where the doer of deeds could have done them better. The credit belongs to the man who is actually in the arena, whose face is marred by dust and sweat and blood; who strives valiantly; who errs, who comes short again and again, because there is no effort without error and shortcoming; but who

does actually strive to do the deeds; who knows great enthusiasms, the great devotions; who spends himself in a worthy cause; who at the best knows in the end the triumph of high achievement, and who at the worst, if he fails, at least fails while daring greatly, so that his place shall never be with those cold and timid souls who neither know victory nor defeat."

It's More Than Intuition

What is true about my entrepreneurial journey, and yours is, passion can get you part of the way, but it takes a lot more to take you all the way.

It takes more than intuition to be a great entrepreneur leader. Intuition without facts to back up your thinking could be a recipe for disaster. I've started more than one business only to find that I would never be successful until I became strategic in my thinking, understood the needs of the people I serve and implemented an action plan based on the knowledge acquired.

Analytics, coupled with intuition, provide a way forward. Analytics enhances decision-making when using clear data points. Data helps leaders:

- understand market and economic influences
- make a case for what's working [or not working]
- improve efficiency and indicate where cost-cutting is necessary
- identify and clarify risk management
- detect patterns so leaders can anticipate change

To go above and beyond the competition, leaders must detect and predict trends. If you're a small start-up, you may not have an analyst in your back pocket to help identify trends. Size does not exempt you from asking relevant questions. Although you cannot always predict the future, as leaders, we can use captured data to advance our learning and help prepare for the future.

Entrepreneurs see where and what efforts should be worked by asking questions and conducting research.

Companies like Yahoo, Microsoft, Amazon, eBay, even your local grocery store collect data for business planning but may use it in different ways. Although not everyone may be positioned to use fancy technology and have data scientists in their corner to analyze quantitative data, there are things you can do to get a sense of what the market will bear.

Where might you get this information? Publications, industry influencers, trend reports, customer feedback, focus groups, user engagement, and observations. Having a data-informed approach with *some* information is better than having no information at all.

Although existing businesses with longevity have access to significant analytics, this does not mean that they will be more successful than a start-up enterprise. The bar is set higher because the need to scale is greater for the start-up.

The Metric That Matters

Start-ups have to be ten times better and be more creative, strategic, and aggressive in the process. The object is for the start-up to understand where the customer's pain is coming from, and find a quicker, more successful solution than the current market competitor.

There are many unknowns in the start-up phase. Digging in and through data to find opportunity to grow a product or company comes with challenges. It may be hard to determine where to locate data, or what determines if the data is useful. Evidence-based metrics change that. Start-ups should be learning as much as possible and steer away from assumptions. Leaders must look under their assumptions, realizing their thinking may be skewed.

Metrics can be informal or formal, internal, or external. Different metrics are used at different organizational stages. The early to high growth phase is prudent to identify roles, encourage communication, and distinguish how initiatives are handled. Typical lean companies look "through the eyes of the customer" to evaluate their systems and processes, deciding what is valuable and viable. Each of my interviews noted this importance.

A good metric is comprised of finding a number that identifies the change you seek, is understandable, a rate or ratio, and changes the current behavior. Alistair Croll and Benjamin Yosovitz, authors of *Lean Analytics,* suggest to capture everything, although focus on what's important; the *one metric* that matters. For each of the entrepreneurs I spoke to, what mattered was different. What matters is dependent on the product or service you provide, along with your industry. A good rule of thumb is to take a stroll outside your industry to gather the information that is relevant.

Trying to do too much at once, or devoting too much time, energy, and financial resources on low impact activities is not suggested. Drill down to what will impact your progress, add value, and leads you to a competitive advantage. As you go through the motions, remember, begin with the end in mind. Focus on the initial data and the decisions that come from that, but understand what happens in-between.

Fact-based and behavioral-based marketing are tactics big and small brands use to categorize trends in the marketplace. These tactics transform the shopping experience for customers. These tactics also promote organizational strategies for growth. Think about it. Every time you swipe a grocery store loyalty card or use a store sponsored credit card, data is collected and used to track spending habits, identify shopping trends, and even depict the times of the month you, the consumer shops. Each time I click on Amazon, a suggestion based on my purchase or search history is populated. Have you noticed your Facebook feed reflects your internet browsing? Big Brother is watching.

It's Time To KIS[S]

Now that you know you *are* creative, and just maybe, you have an idea that might be as great as the Post-it Note, what's next? You've got to **keep it simple** [stupid]! We've all heard this at some point in our life, but for the entrepreneur, The Simple Plan can be a light bulb moment.

The book, *The Myths of Innovation* cuts through the hype and offers a priceless approach.

The Simple Plan suggests:

1. Pick a project and start doing *something*
2. Focus on being good
3. If you work with others, you need leadership and trust
4. If you work with others and things are not going well, make the team smaller

5. Be happy about interesting mistakes

Keeping your approach simple proves to be viable. Breaking the big picture down into bite-size chunks may be the difference between the success or failure of your plan.

The Right Fit Innovators

Being strong and courageous bleeds over into the life of a leader. Dr. Gary Oster imparts, "Innovation requires immense courage." Innovators are constantly swimming against the current.[12]It takes courage to allow followers autonomy or to shoulder responsibility when things do not go as planned.[13] As followers and contributors in the workplace see a visible, courageous leader, they too will be more courageous about exercising creativity and innovation.

Fostering creativity and innovation is done through agile organizations whose leadership is on board.[14]CEOs who do not demand innovation and are resistant to a culture that fosters idea stretching, active participation, willingness to fail, or offer rewards toward the creative process are missing the 21st-century organizational mark for growth.[15]

Moreover, senior leaders must be *focused* on innovation. If senior leaders are only inquiring about sales, reduction projects, and inventory turns, the focus is not on innovation. Because of this, the organization will focus on what the executive considers important.[16]It's up to leadership to hold other senior leaders accountable for innovation growth and push this down and throughout the organization. This produces a culture of creativity and innovation.

An entrepreneur leader cannot just say they want to employ creative people to journey with them; opportunity must be *created*. When hiring for innovation, hiring the wrong people may be in order. Yes, the wrong people.

While hiring the wrong people may seem like a step backward, according to research, this "backward" hiring strategy often finds the right people. Bringing in those who seem "wrong" brings in people who generate higher levels of innovation and creativity, challenge the status quo, and thus increase creativity and diversity.[17]These hiring objectives begin with a leader's clear understanding of what they are

44

looking to innovate, and what approach is needed to get the right people on board.[18] The search for talent must include looking for those with divergent or "backward" thinking.

Leadership must recognize intelligence and creativity are different.[19] As leaders assemble their people and see their human talent through a new unique lens, their offering to the organization becomes an artistic expression, and organizations flourish.

Yes! Yes! Yes!

Entrepreneurship has become a symbol of creativity and innovation, driving economic growth. The entrepreneur revolution is displayed around the world, yet it is an underutilized capability, and often an unthinkable reach for many. Entrepreneur leaders are a different kind of breed. They're passionate and have learned to look for a gap to fill. They're not always the most educated or have the greatest resources, but they find what they need to turn thought into action. They understand every "no" makes the inventor, entrepreneur, or staff member, closer to a *yes* when passion and perseverance are present.

At the end of my interviews, I asked each leader the question, "if you could, would you do this all over again?" There was consensus with the word YES! All the struggles, slammed doors, questioning if they would be able to provide for their family, still led to an overwhelming, yes. Each leader would re-take the entrepreneurial journey, this time, more intelligently. The leaders I interviewed learned priceless lessons along the way, ones that aren't always in the textbooks or the conversations they had early on.

There's a certain level of excitement that is undeniable when you speak to a passionate, driven, entrepreneur leader. My interviews make me want to learn how to spell the word *entrepreneur* without getting the red spell-check every time, and practice pronouncing it instead of avoiding the word or fumbling over it. Why? Because I am an entrepreneur. And maybe, just maybe, I've heightened your desire to take a closer look at the endless possibilities that are waiting for *you*.

Best wishes on your entrepreneurial endeavor!

The Coaching Corner

1. What do you see as the pros and cons of entrepreneurship?
2. When was a time you gave yourself *permission* to explore and expand your creativity?
3. What inspires you to create? To innovate?
4. If you could design an environment to help foster your creativity, what would it look like?
5. How does your organizational culture promote creativity and innovation?
6. What can you do to capture data to guide your venture?
7. What are your current or potential customer pain points?
8. How can you tap into those pain points?
9. How do you celebrate your successes?
10. What is the biggest takeaway from this chapter?

Chapter 4

Leading Through Temptation

"We are what we repeatedly do; excellence then is not an act, but a habit."
~Will Durant

Over time, leadership has proven to be one of the most sought-after and valued activities with numerous theoretical approaches. Leadership has also been misunderstood and misguided. In the process of trying to be leaders, many have lost their way as their values are set aside, and their true north became skewed. An executive title is only as good as the leader who wears it. Strength, Courage, confidence, and a character of excellence helps deter *acting* upon temptation.

I've met high-powered leaders who give the word leadership a bad name. Perhaps you have experienced this too?

Demonstrations of power, privilege, and entitlement are damaging. As a country, we have witnessed accomplished leaders wear their titles with great pride, yet the only place they have led their organizations is into the courtroom or into the ground. In a world full of darkness, these demonstrations are reality. Instead of selfless service-in-action, leaders are serving wealth, power, and greed. This darkness blinds leaders and motivates them toward unethical, toxic, and fraudulent behaviors.

Would you be surprised to learn 1 out of 7 large public companies commit fraud every year? According to 2015 research found in the *Journal of Finance*, fraudulent activity costs shareholders, and the consumer $380 billion a year.

Is the United States the America our founding fathers envisioned, or has it become a petri dish of contaminated leaders? In the last decade, mismanaged organizations and corporate and government scandals have been on the rise. These scandals have led the way to financial disasters that cost more than a few high-profile executives their reputation. In the name of power and prestige, leaders have turned a blind eye to ethical standards and a code of personal conduct.

Our news headlines recount corruption, embarrassment, lies, inappropriate behavior, and cover-ups. I often find myself in disbelief as I read of yet another senior leader or government official getting caught with their hands in the cookie jar or in some cases, literally, with their pants down.

Sadly, we continue to witness misguided steps across diverse industries. It is not surprising to hear of leaders who have been compelled to commit crimes for nothing more than personal gain and then back-peddling in their defense.

During the last decade, Americans have taken a front seat to witness political scandals emerge in the headlines. Consider former New York Governor Elliot Spitzer, caught in the midst of a prostitution ring in 2008.[20] Interestingly, this same man was the white-collar crime-stopper of the Enron era in his position as Attorney General for the state of New York. Another example is former US Congressman Anthony Weiner, who was forced to resign from Congress in 2011 over a "sexting" incident that led to a conviction for the same behavior.[21]

The laundry list of political errors continued during the 2016 United States Presidential election as the infamous unauthorized email server and deleted emails of Democratic Presidential candidate Hillary Clinton made the headlines. The Republicans have had their fair share of troubles. As of this writing, the seemingly never-ending alleged collusion with Russia sound bite, payoffs of hush money, and immunity granting proposals fill social media and news channels daily.

The United States continued to be divided as scandalous behavior, and sexual assault allegations surfaced just days before Republican Supreme Court nominee, Brett Kavanagh's confirmation vote in September 2018. Kavanagh was sworn in as the nation's 114th Supreme Court Justice October 6, 2018, just hours after the Senate voted 50 to 48 to approve the nominee.

In 2016-2017, we watched the sexual assault cases of America's favorite TV father of the 1980's, Bill Cosby, and movie mogul Henry Weinstein take center stage. Media figures from Fox News, CBS, and

NBC joined the growing list of high-profile individuals being suspended or fired amidst harassment scandals.

Resignations and terminations due to mismanaged leadership are widespread. Decision-makers in the auto industry have participated in a walk of shame. Three Takata executives who were charged with wire fraud and falsifying safety reports on their airbags did not make sound judgments.[22]

The 2016 Office of Oversight and Investigations report reflect the faulty airbags have killed at least seventeen people.[23] A January 17, 2018, Associated Press report states this number rose to at least twenty-one when a Florida woman sustained a fractured skull from bursting shrapnel. She died from a faulty airbag. By June of that same year, the total rose to 24. Recalls continue to be released across several automakers as death and injury numbers rise.

The charges for Takata come on the heels of six executives from Volkswagen being indicted in an emissions scandal that affected 11 million vehicles around the globe.[24][25]

Toyota saw its share of embarrassment as the first Western female senior executive was arrested after suspicions of violating the Narcotics Control Act by importing Oxycodone to Japan in 2015. This executive was released and resigned from her position with Toyota[26][27]

The medical and pharmaceutical industry has been scrutinized as the rise in opioid abuse, and heroin overdoses climbed in 2015-2016. Perdue Pharma, Teva, Johnson & Johnson, and medical providers who continue to write prescriptions for pain management have come into the spotlight as opioid-related deaths continue to rise.

The National Survey on Drug Use, along with other supporting data from 2017, indicates 47,000 Americans died from an opioid overdose. These overdoses were from prescription drugs, but also heroin and synthetic cousin, Fentanyl. Research indicates about 80% of heroin users began with prescription opioids. Without responsible legislation and implementing change, our country will continue to mourn loss of life.

In the sports industry, our country was saddened, and in disbelief as the survivors of former USA Olympics national team doctor Larry Nassar, told the world their story. Nassar leveraged power and position to gain trust then exploit numerous patients. In January 2018, a 175-year prison sentence was handed down to this serial child molester.

Church congregations across America have not been spared from incredulous acts of deception. These seemingly safe houses of worship have become seedy headline news. We've watched and read of leaders from around the country meeting with accusations and for some, charged and tried for immoral behavior and unthinkable acts. Although some denominations and congregations have suffered more than others, acts of immorality continue to leave damage and heartache in their wake for survivors.

Scandal and corruption cross all industries with remnants spilling down and seeping into the culture of many organizations. Leaders are called to a higher standard. To whom much is given, much is required.

Managing power and responsibility begins at the top with senior leaders positioned to model what ethical conduct looks like. Accountability, responsibility, and transparency were lacking in the above examples. Where guilt was determined, careless executive and self-leadership were demonstrated.

Beyond a "playbook," leaders must implement leadership principles that align with excellence.

For the high-powered executives and representatives in their industry who were charged, more was asked. Did they act with courage and moral fortitude, or were they blinded by their position or fame? Sadly, it's not just the industry, organization, or the employee who suffers a loss due to a personal lapse in judgment. The reach extends to the families who face embarrassment, humiliation, and heartache.

Having power and privilege with no transparency or no checks and balances in place has a trickle-down effect inside organizations. The key for leaders is in learning to *manage* their power. Whether you lead an organization, a team, your family, or yourself, the leadership you provide on a day-to-day basis should be measured. Incorporating principles of excellence motivates leaders to reach above and beyond the existing norm. Excellence as a leadership style takes having a strong, unchanging moral and ethical code.

Freedom of Choice

Lean in. Leaders are to appear and act appropriately at all times, not just when others are looking. For those who know the story of the Garden of Eden, you may remember the snake *tempted* it did not force. The lesson here is clear. It is by *choice* that we disobey.

For 2,500 years, shared values have been taught throughout cultures by using the Golden Rule.[28] Although the Golden Rule is universally explained, research identifies environmental and psychological factors to determine whether or not leaders act on temptations. There are psychological implications that drive thoughts into actions[29] that then form social norm acceptance.[30] The personal value system that individuals hold indicates whether or not they engage in unethical behaviors, as well as having the "opportunity" to act.[31]

The opportunity to act is demonstrated in entertaining research of the '60s-'70s. Have you ever heard of the marshmallow experiment? This longitudinal work was initiated by a Stanford professor that depicts delayed gratification and motivation. The children who delayed gratification and chose not eat the marshmallow so that they could have two marshmallows [later] were found to have better SAT scores, less substance abuse, better social skills, less likelihood to have obesity.

Decision-making styles, personal values, and personality traits are often influencers of motivation. However, leaders are also lured toward unethical behavior based on incentives that lead to personal gain. In other words, some leaders make a choice to eat the marshmallow. Incentives may come in the form of commissions and bonuses based on quotas. Having a solid ethical and moral code provides necessary boundaries. These boundaries are the gatekeepers of your ethical and moral code.

If you're not quite sure what the difference is between ethics and morals, you are not alone. Many people use the two interchangeably. The Greek origin of the word ethics is *ethos*. Ethics are principles deemed acceptable based on society or an organization. Ethics are principles and rules to live by.

The word moral comes from the ancient Roman language, Latin, and means *custom.* How we apply ethical principles describes our morality. Because we are given free will to choose, morals are dependent upon what we as an individual believe is right and true. Moral law is defined as general, unchanging rules of living rightly. Our moral standard is based in and assessed by our own account of right or wrong. In an organizational context, the ethical code of conduct will determine right or wrong.

The Right Thing To Do?

I was taught at an early age to do the right thing because it is the right thing to do *and* treat others like I want to be treated. Still, I have struggled, stumbled, and had my share of sleepless nights over decisions I have made, never really knowing at the time if the final decision was the right one. When I came to realize both personal and business decisions could be handled using the same moral code, decision-making became a lot less complicated.

Leaders are faced with ethical decisions and dilemmas, often getting caught in the middle of differing personal, shareholder, and stakeholder morals. This can be conflicting. The most difficult decisions that a leader will struggle with are the *right versus right* decisions. These decisions are the ones where both options may equally be the best choice, yet only one outcome can prevail. Being able to weigh the dilemma on a moral scale will produce a better result, remembering; *the right decision is not always the popular one.*

Making well thought out decisions is hard and takes more than just doing the math on paper to get to an answer. It may require some heart. My business venture as a social entrepreneur is a great example of a *know when to say when, right versus right* decision. Accepting the reality to close the doors remains the most difficult leadership decision I have made to date. The heart and mind power-struggle was excruciating.

Aristotle, the Greek philosopher, suggests personal judgment can be trusted; yet, the determinant is based on the amount of sound moral character one possesses. I would add decision-making is also dependent on the psychological and emotional state a person is in at the time.

Have you ever heard that saying, "go with your heart, but take your brain with you?" Many leaders have made decisions based solely on emotions *or* strictly on the balance sheet. Each comes with consequences.

The heart and mind are both necessary for leaders to inspire, encourage, and instill a culture of sound values for their organization. Nevertheless, leaders may still lose sleep over decision-making that affects people negatively, even if the decision is the right thing to do.

We are all human, with feelings, emotions, and egos. There are times leaders will need to make snap judgments, and those who are good and intuitively strong by nature may not have difficulty in this area.

However, there are times when there's power in the pause, taking time to think through a decision even for the quick-witted. Once the words leave your lips, the text button is pushed, or the email is sent; right or wrong, the outcome is yours to own. This doesn't mean you can't change your mind and make things right, but a solid decision based on sound judgment aligns with best practices for leadership excellence.

You may argue that business ethics is an oxymoron. I would agree that some organizations have made ruthless decisions to gain wealth, people, and ideas through less than noble acts. Leaders are moral agents, entrusted to act on others' behalf and be stewards of their organizations.[32]Having an ethical organization with moral individuals in the workplace is a vital principle of excellence. Most likely, when your moral code does not align with your organization, problems will ultimately arise.

Have you ever been faced with a moral decision in the workplace? In 1997, after alerting the Drug Enforcement Agency of a wrongdoing taking place in the office where I worked, I became what is known as a *whistleblower*.

Risky Business

Whistleblowing is not uncommon in a world full of corruption. When there are negative actions and behaviors in the workplace, an ethical response is demonstrated by communicating the wrongdoing to internal or external authorities. Still, whistleblowing does not come without personal and professional risk.

> *Ethical guidelines are only as good as they are executed and enforced.*

Whistleblowers are motivated by individual, organizational, or social reasons.[33]

While some whistleblowers do so for notoriety or to achieve other individual or material gains, others seek to protect society.

My experience was based on providing protection to the patients and staff at the medical office where I was employed. In this small-town office, the medical provider had a problem with writing scripts and self-medicating. These erroneous acts put the welfare of his patients in harm's way to which I had a front-row seat to witness.

I mentioned earlier that I was taught to do the right thing because it is the right thing to do. Knowing this and living this are two different things. I had turned my head one too many times, all in an effort to keep my job and hope that things would change. The fact remained; nothing changed. The only thing I could change is how I responded to knowing and watching the failed leadership unfold. I had to act.

I responded by quitting my job and providing the authorities with the information that was needed to strip the doctor of his license until he received the help he needed.

Courageous leaders go to battle over what they believe in. Although I acted, my courage to act cost me. It wasn't just my employment. It was also the relationships of those who did not understand why I acted. I lived in fear of retaliation.

My fear eventually lifted, and I was able to clearly see that my actions aligned with my intent to protect.

The doctor went into treatment and eventually practiced medicine again. I never spoke or saw him after I left his employment.

Whistleblowing on a grander, more public scale was demonstrated by the actions of VA (Veterans Administration) employee, Paula Dewenter.

In 2014, Dewenter exposed the corrosive culture in the nation's health care system. Dewenter reported secret waiting lists and inaccurate death and suicide data at the VA's Carl T. Hayden Medical Center in Arizona.[34] Subsequent investigations of the VA showed supervisors in seven states received instructions to manipulate scheduling to show performance measures were met. Statistics from March 2016 indicated over 480,000 veterans across the country were waiting a month or longer for care.[35] The culture of the VA health care system was in need of immediate personnel, policy, and full culture overhaul.

With time, organizations evolve and should continually seek to modify and implement change efforts related to ethics.[36] The VA healthcare system was overdue and should have been changed long ago. When clear policies or a code of ethics is in place, *behaviors can be modified to align with the organization.* However, ethical guidelines are only as good as they are executed and enforced. If leaders are not willing to allocate training to advance and educate their people on organizational guidelines or choose not to deliver consequences to repeat offenders, the corporate culture will suffer.

Many leaders lean into unethical behavior based on high-performance standards and intense ambition. These leaders lose sight of what is right and instead gravitate toward self-serving personal pleasure and the dark side of leadership. Those who display a higher moral identity are those who will act in conjunction with moral principles and values. Their actions will align with the ethical and moral principles of excellence.

Habits of Excellence

Developing sound judgment is part of crafting a character of excellence. Your character is at the cornerstone of leadership. Ask yourself: What kind of person do I genuinely want to be? What am I portraying to the world?

Having a character of excellence encompasses the right motives and intentions in everything you do because you have a desire to do so. If you are open to question your character, it means you are open to being crafted. Sometimes the crafting process hurts because it involves change. Change is painful and uncomfortable, but change can also bear great fruit. As leaders surrender to being molded as a virtuous leader of excellence, a transformation process of character begins. Character becomes matured when leaders purposefully design, align and position their character change efforts towards excellence. Once matured, character runs deep and is steadfast.[37] Leaders become new.

Valuable Virtues

The continuous path to strive for leadership maturity and goodness of character is linked to the virtuous leader. Research demonstrates the word *virtue* has many definitions. The word itself comes from the Greek word *excellence;* hence, leaders are called to be habitually and intentionally virtuous.[38]

Virtues are habits of excellence, *patterns* of behavior that create what we think, feel, and how we act in accordance with the characteristics that make us better human beings.[39] Better human beings become better leaders. Better leaders do not live by worldly standards of perfection, but rather seek excellence in all they do.

> *The virtuous leader's authenticity becomes their natural repeated response in and outside the workplace.*

Excellence by design is a daily act of knowing, being, and doing. Leading with excellence is a way of life. Excellence is a leadership style that embraces a call to go above and beyond.

Excellence requires leaders to be more than adequate, give more than take, and be at peace as they let go of power and control. By letting go, leaders make room to empower, build, and transform their workplace.

Designing our lives as leaders must rest on a set of virtues that form the basis for our entire life. We cannot determine if a person is virtuous based on their physical appearance. Rather, it is in the outward public display of those virtues that demonstrate if they are present.[40]

Virtues are guided by imitation and observation.[41] Virtues may or may not be innate; can be learned when practiced, are a character trait, are contextually embedded; and are voluntarily expressed. Our character development begins with our moral decision-making patterned after years of confronting and deciding what we see as moral or immoral.[42] To be virtuous takes a considerable degree of consistency, determined effort to train the brain toward living and leading with excellence.

Being virtuous is behavioral, and collectively, makes up what is presumed to be good character. According to author Craig Johnson,[43] virtues are ingrained in a leader, shape their actions and behaviors, are not situational, and give the leader the ability to live a more fulfilling life. The virtuous leader's authenticity becomes their natural repeated response in and outside the workplace.

The contributions of Greek philosophers Aristotle and Plato formed a consensus set of Cardinal Virtues that are "hinged on which all the other virtues are hung."[44]

Cardinal virtues include prudence, courage, justice, and temperance (self-control). Although Cardinal Virtues include what would be a demonstration of virtuous living, there are additional virtues that are instrumental in living a virtuous life. Researchers and scribes have contributed and expanded upon virtues to include: hope, faith, love, forgiveness, humility, joy, patience, and charity. Leadership excellence by design incorporates *all* virtues as a way to raise the standards of best-practice leadership.

Volatile Vices

Virtue, character, and responsibility are the backbone of virtuous ethics that guide a virtuous leader to take the right action because of the desire to do right.[45] It is through virtuous living and leading that we inherit excellence in our workplace.

When a leader is at the crossroads of virtues and vices, she or he has a choice to make. When leaders lose focus, they become complacent; often believing they can hide their indiscretions.[46]

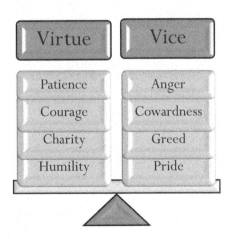

Leaders create confusion for those they lead as they become entangled with vices that result in behaviors inconsistent with virtuous character.

Virtues and vices may be understood differently based on culture. This lack of clarity may present obstacles for leaders, followers, relational partners, and contributors in the workplace.

As demonstrated by the short-list of examples on the previous page, for every virtue, there is a vice, a practice made by personal choice that create behaviors which are not in line with habits of excellence. Vices are patterns of wrongdoing.

Imagine the workplace of a virtuous leader.

Now, imagine the same workplace with a leader demonstrating acts of vices.

The vices that have captured the minds of influential 21st-century leaders are the same as what leaders have experienced over the last several thousand years. The repetition of historical themes is still present today.

Interestingly, the leaders and organizations named earlier in this chapter who lost their moral compass are no different than what is outlined in the oldest, best-selling historical manuscript ever written, the Bible. The actors in the script and the time period which they took place are all that has changed.

Leaders make bad choices. Regardless of the century which they lead, leaders are faced with the choice to lead and act rightly or be overcome by the power of vices. Therefore, leaders must safeguard themselves and their organization from corrupt behavior. When leaders focus on virtuous living and leading, excellence follows.

The Coaching Corner

1. What corruption or wrong-doings have you witnessed in your organization? What part did you play, if any?
2. What is the hardest right versus right work-related decision you've had to make?
3. Would you make the same decision today? Why or why not?
4. What virtues and vices do you struggle with [or have struggled with]?
5. What is one step that will help you [or helped you] move past the struggle?
6. Who can help hold you accountable as you move forward?
7. When "what is right" is in question, what does your organization use as an ethical measuring stick?
8. What do you use as your moral measuring stick?

Chapter 5

Leading With Safeguards

"Transparency is needed to create trust, and also to create dialogue."
~Julie Sweet

When you live and lead by principles of excellence, you become more than a leader. You become a *best practice* living example. Leading with excellence means you choose to implement a measuring stick. This measuring stick inspires others to go above and beyond what is expected. It also identifies boundaries and safe zones.

Organizational safeguards like those listed on the following page can be successfully drafted, executed, and used strategically to guide ethical decision-making and create habits of excellence.

Safeguards offer ethical direction for leaders and organizational partners. Safeguards are to be *practiced,* not put in a binder, placed in a drawer or hidden in a closet. Simply stated, safeguards are in place to keep you and your organization safe!

It is in individual practice, and obedience to excellence where transformation lives and organizational change occurs. As leaders lean in and discern how to create excellence in the workplace by providing guidance, it eliminates the question of what is wrong and replaces it with what is right and true.

The answers to what is right and true illuminate the leader's example throughout the organization, allowing everyone to become less about living by rules, and more about embracing the transformational process safeguards for your organization afford.

The world *is* watching. Every move you make is sending a message that outwardly speaks to who you are, what you stand for, and more importantly, what you value individually and organizationally.

Organizations set the example and build an aligned culture by creating a shared vision with shared expectations. Increasing motivation toward integrity and ethical decision-making through a rewards system is imperative. This creates a positive culture.

Are you acknowledging the contributors who are kind, obedient, and align their work practice with the practice of excellence?

As leaders, we must not forget to honor those who work and lead rightly. Time spent acknowledging whom and what is righteous will present motivated, dedicated contributors. Raising and rewarding ethical awareness [not just commissions for sales or new customers] creates a culture of workplace excellence.

Gate-Keepers & Guard Rails

The ethical and moral integrity of our organizations must be monitored. Human Resource (HR) leaders are the gatekeepers who ensure credibility and organizational excellence.[47] Ethical and legal standards are an essential aspect of a code of conduct, however, these standards must be enforced.

A code of conduct goes beyond a mission and values statement, or employee handbook. A code of conduct is a supplement to both. For the organization, displaying the code of conduct and values statement teaches your employees you take your beliefs seriously. It allows your current workforce to know where the guardrails are. In addition, these guardrails communicate a message to the external environment. The beliefs the organization exhibits may be the determining factor for potential employment candidates and business partners who will decide if your company is a good match….or not.

Without question, organizations blindly ignore followers who are unethical and choose to go beyond the guardrails. Leaders are warned not to steal and make right any wrong behavior. So, I ask, do you turn a blind eye to the wrongs happening within your workplace?

Turning a blind eye at the medical office early in my career in the hope there would be change does not make the act right. Nor does stealing the Post-It Notes to fill for your home office drawer. When you begin to compromise the little things, inevitably, big things will follow. The gradual progression of temptation and compromise is a slippery slope for leaders.

Organizations cannot sacrifice ethics and responsibilities to initiate self-satisfying acts of unethical behavior. For it is the narrow, moral, obedient gate that leaders must enter. Self-serving leaders do not protect their followers or their organizations; they protect their agenda.[48]

Many employees feel leaders are unethical and underhanded in their business dealings. Such actions, in turn, penetrate the organization and clone the leaders' behaviors into the corporate culture, creating unscrupulous followers.[49]

In a world where the bottom line is often the dictator of actions and reactions, establishing shared core values is essential. Shared core values create by-products of higher profits, increased trust, higher performance levels, and greater job satisfaction.[50] Leaders have the opportunity to unify their people and model the way for the future with moral solidarity.

Moral Solidarity

Leaders are faced with a barrage of moral challenges. Our moral judgments are based on our moral experiences, social relationships, and obedience [or lack thereof] to a moral code. Obedience to a moral code takes an uninterrupted submission to excellence. Our world has seen many leaders replaced, failing to uphold their role. Failure originates from burnout, stress, or impairment of analytical and creative thinking. Vices of alcohol, drugs, illicit sex… fast track moral derailment, and a failed leadership experience.

In our diverse organizations, moral solidarity is necessary. For leaders, moral solidarity takes navigating through different perspectives bringing differing world-views into a collective moral compass. In the end, regardless of all the credos, training, and rewards, we are each responsible for our individual choices, which must be acknowledged and explained.

When leaders fail to act responsibly, re-adjusting the moral compass is necessary to get back on track. This moral compass must be more than a symbolic image, but express shared wisdom that becomes communal throughout the organization. Admitting your wrongs is part of the re-adjustment process.

The Other "F" Word

Do you admit when you're wrong or have wronged someone? Have you ever had someone come to you and apologize or ask for forgiveness? Leaders who design their lives and organizations for excellence are aware of their faults and work to correct them. They stand firm, having no tolerance for unethical behavior in an organization, even if *they* are the offender. A leader must understand the problem, repent, and realign with the ethical duties of their position to improve the organization's attainment of excellence.[51]

Although it may be difficult for any leader to repent for wrongs, it demonstrates excellent strength and obedience to a moral code. Leaders are not exempt from misdeeds, whether to or from others. Leaders need to have accountability within their organization when things go wrong.[52]

Imagine a senior leader humbly showing remorse for a wrong committed. I'm not talking about the word 'sorry' that people throw around that has little or no meaning. I'm talking about having the heartbeat of excellence and a truthful tongue that tells a person or an entire organization the wrong that has been committed, asks for forgiveness, and makes amends.

When a leader lives this example before followers and contributors, leaders are viewed as genuine, someone who struggles [just like them], and is not untouchable. We are all human. We all make mistakes.

Transformation is found in self-correction and forgiveness. It takes courage to come forward and confess a transgression, and takes moral conviction to stay the course and not be a repeat offender.

In a news conference, former New York Governor Elliot Spitzer said, "I have disappointed and failed to live up to the standard I expected of myself. I must now dedicate some time to regain the trust of my family."

At the court hearing for disgraced US Congressman Anthony Weiner, he explained, "I hit rock bottom...through treatment, I found the courage to take a moral inventory of my defects....I accept full responsibility for my conduct."[53]

Conversely and disappointing many, former VA Secretary Robert McDonald missed the mark as he compared the wait times for our veterans to the lines at Disneyland. "If my comments led any Veterans to believe that I, or the dedicated workforce I am privileged to lead, don't take that noble mission seriously, I deeply regret that. Nothing can be further from the truth."[54]

Perdue Pharma, the makers of OxyContin, provided a less than satisfactory response to the overdose epidemic as callous remarks were uncovered by their senior leaders. In response to the statements made, Connecticut Attorney General William Tong calls the remarks "outrageous comments that show an utter disregard for human life."[55]

When leaders set a moral example by outwardly repenting and making amends for wrong behavior, they are more apt to regain the trust of others. Trust earned transforms a leader and the organization. To ignore the significance of past errors and how they affected others will indicate the leader is not ready for transformation.

Principles of excellence, including repentance, are demonstrated in many cultures as a way to give insight and positively impact the leader's relationship with their people and with shareholders.[56]

Through repentance, trust is rebuilt, and as the leader strives to improve, commitment is re-established. On the contrary, when leaders are dishonest and do not repent, they lose the respect of others. The leader is seen as unreliable and undependable, therefore weakening relationships.[57]

To repent, a leader must not just want to change, but put actions behind the desired change. When a leader seeks to understand her or his faults and implement change, a cycle of learning is created, and their performance as a leader improves.[58]

In the name of leadership, there are many decisions and actions a leader must take. Is there someone you need to forgive or ask for forgiveness? We are all human and make mistakes. Maybe the person you need to forgive is yourself. Being able to offer and accept forgiveness is part of demonstrating leadership excellence.

The Coaching Corner

1. As a leader, how do you demonstrate being a living example to a world that's watching?
2. How are senior leaders partnering with HR to ensure compliance with organizational safeguards?
3. How are safeguards enforced in your organization? What needs to change?
4. Who holds *you* accountable? Is it enough?
5. How do you honor those who work and lead rightly?
6. How accurate is your moral compass? Be honest.
7. What compass adjustments could make you a stronger leader?
8. Whom do you need to say the words, "I'm sorry?"
    When will you have that conversation?

Chapter 6

Leading Talent Development & Engagement

"Your talent is God's gift to you. What you do with it is your gift back to God."
~Leo Buscaglia

If you're an entrepreneur or solo-entrepreneur, no people to manage, or think talent management, development, and engagement are just buzzwords, don't skip ahead. Managing your own talent, development, and engagement is just as, if not more critical than managing others. The areas addressed in this chapter are essential to your success as a leader and bringing others into the leadership excellence fold regardless of the number of direct reports you have.

If I were to ask, what's your organization's most valuable asset, what would you say? The incredible piece of real estate you purchased, your patent, trademark, or other intellectual property you own? Or, maybe it's the brilliant technology you bought that allows you to get more done in less time with fewer people?

When it comes down to it, technology, real estate and patents all have a place, however, they will never take the place of your human talent; those who walk the halls, sit in cubicles, are a phone call, text, or email away, and stand front and center when you need them most.

Your masterfully crafted people are and forever will be your ultimate competitive advantage and your greatest asset! This advantage exponentially increases when leaders embrace and design for excellence. Designing a purposeful approach generates stronger, more satisfied employees. In the process, your organization will grow its bottom line.

HR Trends

Organizations are being judged less on traditional metrics of quality and financial performance, but rather, on relational capital and the impact on society at large.[59] The contributors in your workplace, those who bring their best to your organization, are looking for virtuous leaders.

According to *Deloitte's 2018 Human Capital Trends* report, leaders are being challenged to operate with transparency, be credible, consistent, and trustworthy. The survey participants seek leaders who reach into their organizations as well as out into their communities. These important aspects found in the report are equally as important as the previous year's findings.

In 2017, the Deloitte University Press survey[60] revealed the top six trends as:

1. Organization of the future (88%)
2. Careers and learning (83%)
3. Talent Acquisition (81%)
4. Employee Experience (79%)
5. Performance Management (78%)
6. Leadership (78%)

Deloitte argues organizations must move toward adequately funding HR to attract a qualified talent pool. Senior leader buy-in for this partnership is crucial because developing talent takes resources. Yes, that does include financial resources, but it goes beyond that. Resources include the right people. When done right, clarity flows from leader to HR, ensuring alignment of organizational needs while creating a talent pool to deliver on the leader's vision.

Talent recruiting and acquisition has changed dramatically over the last several years as technology continues to grow and becomes a staple in the hiring process. When organizations strategically fund their HR initiatives, they have a better chance of attracting *and* retaining key players. As the workforce evolves and generational differences impact our organizations, seeking the latest and greatest recruitment tools and development strategy are needed. However, relationships will remain at the forefront of why people come and why people leave.

Millennial Mayhem?

Jason Dorsey, researcher and President of Center for Generation Kinetics states, generations provide powerful and predictive clues to connect faster and influence others. According to his research, the trend reaches around the world. Therefore, it would be remiss to move on without touching on one of the most significant movements of our time, the Millennials.

What comes to mind when you hear Millennials? For some, it gets an eye roll, for others, the word may spark a sense of pride. Whatever your thoughts on this generation, those born between January 1981 and December 1996[61] have become a fascinating generation to research. As of this writing, Millennials fall between the ages of 23-38.

> *Your masterfully crafted people are and forever will be your ultimate competitive advantage.*

The Millennials are currently the largest working generation. Recruitment efforts to gain talented Millennials look different today than the recruitment practices of previous generations. Since 2014, the number of organizations that utilize social tools to recruit and hire talent has more than doubled.[62]Talent acquisition and approach continues to advance as the current and upcoming generations entering the workforce reach to technology as their first-line method of communication. Products that support a new technological approach to talent acquisition include cognitive tools, gaming, and video.

The Millennial generation has revealed that your title and age do not have to be congruent. This generation is large and in charge! Facebook, Instagram, Snapchat, and Uber all have one thing in common; they have executives and Founders birthed into a generation where regardless of your initial thinking, they have changed the way the world sees leadership.

Although you may think these tech-dependent members of the workforce who embrace and push the limits of innovation push away the importance of relationships, you are wrong.

Millennials understand that fostering relationships is still a necessary role in and outside of the work arena. Though, many times, their relationship building comes in the form of raising awareness by asking, "how can we do things differently?" As a global workforce, we have to ask ourselves, is asking so disparaging? If science and leadership as a theory are to find and end in truth, encouraging differences is essential. Embracing all generational contributions makes for a collective, connective culture.

As Millennials continue to advance their ideas and place on the hierarchy chart, Gen Z [currently ranging from age from 7-22] is close behind as they enter the workforce. Gen Z is also referred to as iGen or Centennials. Many are working fulltime or are completing higher degrees. HR departments around the globe are watching, learning, and advancing creative ways to capture talent based on the individual and the culture of this post Millennial generation.

As with all generations, start and end years for birth are approximate as researchers have no clear definition of when one generation ends and another begins. Therefore, many times, we see overlap. Pew Research defines the generations as follows:

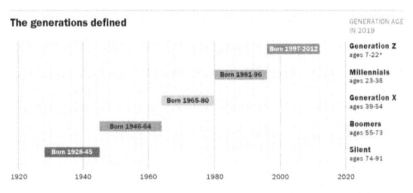

The generations defined

GENERATION AGE IN 2019

					Born 1997-2012	**Generation Z** ages 7-22*
				Born 1981-96		**Millennials** ages 23-38
			Born 1965-80			**Generation X** ages 39-54
	Born 1946-64					**Boomers** ages 55-73
Born 1928-45						**Silent** ages 74-91

| 1920 | 1940 | 1960 | 1980 | 2000 | 2020 |

† No chronological endpoint has been set for this group. For this analysis, Generation Z is defined as those ages 7 to 22 in 2019.

Who's Managing Your Talent?

Managing a talented workforce is not done by chance. Managing a talented workforce is designed. When I think design, I think strategy. When I think strategy, the words of Canadian author and academic professor Henry Mintzberg come to mind. Mintzberg speaks of strategic thinking as *seeing*. To think strategically requires "seeing ahead and behind, seeing above and below, seeing beside and beyond, and seeing it through."[63] So, how do you *see* and manage your talent?

Successful companies employ powerful, creative, work-giving human talent. However, strategy and success do not stop there. Organizations succeed because people enable the organization's success.[64] To gain and retain the best and brightest human talent, leaders must partner with HR to develop a shared delivery system of processes and practices. This partnership links vision, people, and processes that ultimately fill the talent pool.

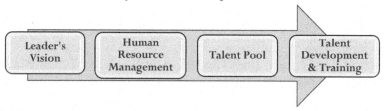

As a leader, it is necessary to openly communicate with your HR leaders to create, set, and sustain a continuous talent pool. The partnership between leaders must be fluid. Communicating and internalizing the leader's vision is only the beginning. A healthy relationship fosters trust as leaders work together to promote effective planning to execute the vision efficiently.

Responsible leaders are concerned with job responsibility, not just job security. Therefore, there is a responsibility for HR to know the pulse and the heartbeat of the organization, its people. The crux of HR leadership is developing HR processes and practices that identify with the organization's objectives, but intersect with employee goals. Think of these goals as development opportunities.

Pigeonholing "Potential"

What is potential? The Merriam-Webster dictionary states potential is "having capacity to become or develop into something" - "latent qualities or abilities that may be developed and lead to future successes." How do you *qualify* potential? Does your qualifying end in truth? If it does, whose truth?

Leaders often refer to those who are being "looked at" and groomed for advancement as high potentials. Although "high potential" is a phrase that is tossed around in today's work environments, it's important to keep in mind "high potential" can be a gray area. More times than not, potential is seen through the eye of the beholder and may not be accurate.

Too often, organizations are pigeonholing talent. We place employees in positions where we think they belong. We pay them low wages.

When employees are pigeonholed, they are never allowed the opportunity to rise *beyond* what you define as their "potential." You also take the chance of losing the employee as they seek employment opportunities elsewhere. People want to use their talent and the gifts they have fully. Pigeonholing your people hinders growth, self-worth, and advancement.

Have you ever been pigeonholed? The practice of pigeonholing occurred during various times in my life. For me, pigeonholing typically showed up when others didn't fully know me and therefore underestimated or discounted my capabilities.

Looking back at my career, I can confidently say I have been pigeonholed more times than not. During my initial meeting with state officials to open the child development center, I was told I wouldn't succeed. The conversation was based on the number of people who said they wanted to open a state-licensed child development center and those who actually see it through. I was judged based on the state representative's experience with others without her knowing my capabilities or drive. I had a vision. I was called forth to proceed. No one was going to change that. After successfully executing the buildout, the center was licensed and open for business.

The practice of pigeonholing was again evident when I began to work on military installations in 2007. Military life has its challenges. Unless a military spouse has an established portable career, finding gainful employment is difficult.

I did not realize when I left the town I was born and raised in to follow my [now] husband; I was putting my professional career temporarily on hold. I found I was at the mercy of the hiring manager who generally needed a warm body to fill a low wage position.

I grew to understand a revolving door of hires was expected, as was the low wage. Why? Because when military orders come, managers know their employees leave everything behind, including their job.

During this period of time, having a bachelor's degree didn't help me. My past civilian work-related successes didn't help me. Imagine,

I went from being a civilian Executive Director of the start-up I founded to a furniture sales associate on a military installation. Starting wage: a meager $7.75 per hour! Nevertheless, this wage did not stop me from giving my best to the organization.

Although I was initially pigeonholed, I received excellent reviews. Within one year, I moved from being a sales associate to entrusted as an inventory control specialist, and then selected to work at the administrative offices for the General Manager. This upward swing improved my hourly wage to $9.45.

My hourly wage doesn't seem like much in a world where [in some states] I could work at a fast-food restaurant for $14 per hour. Still, I was grateful for the opportunity. I finally felt like my foot was in the door for advancement. However, that would-be advancement happened just in time for me to move on to the next military installation.

I expected the transition to Fort Polk, Louisiana, to be clean and uncomplicated. I expected to land a position making at least $9.45. And, after working as the assistant to a GM, I expected never to work retail again. I was wrong. Once again, like many military spouses, I found myself at the bottom rung of the retail ladder. Only this time, it was behind the fine jewelry counter, making a sparkling $7.50 per hour. Yes, I was hired by the same company that promoted me through three positions in a year. And yes, I found myself "demoted" in position and wage. Why? Because they could.

There are lessons in every position I have held. Some to teach and grow me, and some to humble me. The lessons I learned as a military spouse were of humility and acceptance regardless of circumstance. That wasn't the only lesson during this time.

Yes, I was working long, tiring retail hours for a very small hourly wage, but looking back, I was being pruned. The wage I made had been at the forefront of everything. I had let my wage define me until I had a mindset shift. I began seeing my position not as lowly, rather, through the eyes of service to our great American soldiers and their families.

I was blessed each time I listened to stories of how a soldier was planning to propose, or, each time he brought his fiancé or new bride to meet me. My position behind the jewelry counter brought more than I could have expected. There is no amount of money that could take the place of the joy I experienced.

The act of serving regardless of my place on the hierarchy chart would carry through to the final military installation on the island of Oahu. There, I was hired for a 1-year assignment to temporarily serve as an assistant to a division Director before realizing there was a greater plan for my life.

The lessons I learned about humble service and acceptance during my military work career expanded my leadership lens. I learned a paid or unpaid role, leadership, or otherwise did not define the person as "leader." A person is defined as a leader by their mindset, actions, and impact of their delivery.

The act of being pigeonholed during those days didn't make me perform with less excellence. It did, however, create awareness for myself and [hopefully] for those who judged me before knowing me.

Eighteen years after that first meeting with the state, and six years after leaving my position for the Director in Hawaii, equipped with a doctoral degree, advanced experience, and the same drive and executing capabilities, pigeonholing was again evident. This time in a board room full of influencers who questioned my capabilities to create impact for their leadership. At the onset, my ego was [slightly] bruised...I know my capabilities, but the suits sitting in the board room chairs did not—yet. I would need to prove those capabilities. The good news is, I was awarded the contract and have enjoyed repeat business from that prestigious organization.

I have been a surprise to more than a few people over the span of my leadership career, and yes, I have surpassed colleagues with a "Type A personality" that so many organizations feel is imperative for successful leadership outcomes. I am proof that an introvert with a passion and purpose can lead with courage, confidence, and be a successful leader [and so can you].

It's important to remember, developing your people, regardless of their personality "type," will ready your organization for future success and sustainability. If hiring for fit is solely based on "type," you run the risk of having a flawed hiring process and missing out on brilliant talent.

> *A leader is defined by their mindset, actions, and impact of their delivery.*

Developing Talent

Brilliant talent comes in all shapes, sizes, genders, IQ, and level of education. It's up to the organization to foster that brilliance.

Twenty-first-century organizations are required to grow in order to be successful. This means that your people, too, must grow. This takes development. Leadership development ensures organizational readiness, effectiveness, efficiency, and sustainability.

Your organization is made up of uniquely crafted individuals, who are creative, innovative, and filled with purpose. These individuals need an advocate who will clutch the keys and drive leadership development throughout the organization. Are you advocating for yourself *and* your people? Perhaps it is time to begin.

Pew Research Center's, *The State of American Jobs* 2016 report[65] implies the economy has been responsible for reshaping both work and society, which affects how people think about their skills and training. This same research suggests not only is more preparation needed to achieve career success, but 54% of the American's polled feel it "is essential" to continually be upgrading through developing their skills, while 33% say it "is important, but not essential." Only 12% suggest on-going training will "**not** be important."

The research additionally identifies 72% of the respondents stating, "…a lot of responsibility falls on individuals to make sure that they have the right skills and education to be successful in today's economy."

The PEW report is more than analyzing percentages; it uncovers the mindset of today's workforce. The mindset points to the importance and responsibility of the organization to partner with their people. The development needs of your organization are determined through an organizational partnership. Designing a customized approach keeps both the organization and the individual engaged.

Organizations must find the right future-fit that includes staff that is skilled and willing to take on future advancements. Nonetheless, high potentials are only as good as the development opportunities that are offered and successfully take part in. The grooming process is by deliberate design. It's not coincidental, nor left to chance. The likelihood of sustainability across today's diverse organizations increases when development is planned. Remember, everything that is shiny is not gold, and the "best fit" individual for your organization might be found within your existing walls.

Looking Within: Internal Candidates

There may be times when leaders have to go outside their organization to find a suitable candidate. However, it may come with a cost. Organizations may find hiring external candidates has a negative impact on an organization with an already established culture. Though, bringing in an outsider who is aligned with the beliefs, values, and assumptions of the organization may create a significant opportunity for success.[66]

Looking inside the candidate box to your existing talent who are already embedded in a healthy culture may be an answer to the HR call to fill a position. Internal candidates are compared to a kinship. Demonstrations of kinship include solidarity, cooperation, and trust.[67] When leaders look at talent *within* the organization, it fills people with optimism and hope. Internal selections boost morale and loyalty. Offering opportunity and hope to your people allows for future-focused thinking. They begin to look at their work as being part of something bigger than themselves.

Unity happens over time as the leader's vision creates organizational culture. Therefore, internal candidates ought not to be overlooked, and their readiness should not be discounted. Preparing internal candidates appropriately by identifying development efforts is a continuous process.

Increasing your internal leadership development channels isn't rocket science. Like anything else that breeds success, expanding your internal pool of candidates takes finding a process that works. Your process begins with asking questions. The following questions will get you started:

What are our immediate, mission-critical vacancies?

What are our [known] upcoming vacancies [due to promotions, etc.]?

What are the necessary competencies for each position?

Who currently has these competencies, or who can be appropriately aligned and developed accordingly?

Once determined, the process can be adjusted, developed more fully, and repeated as necessary.

The Box-Checker Mentality

I admit I like to check boxes! It helps me stay on track and see what I have accomplished. However, having a box-checker mentality when it comes to delivering and processing HR requirements is another story. Developing talent means more than having your team complete an Individual Development Plan (IDP) as a yearly HR requirement. Completing an IDP was mandatory at an organization I worked for several years ago. I had no idea what it was or why it mattered. When I asked how to complete the IDP, I was told, "just put down a few things where you think you need more training and hand the form in." And so, I did just that.

The answer I received, coupled with inaction and follow-up from the organization, led me to believe the document was nothing more than what I call an HR box-checker. A box-checker is a requirement that is necessary to complete by a specific date, or the department head is "pinged" until completed. This response to an HR requirement is not uncommon for organizations that are flooded with monthly, quarterly, and yearly requirements. As I look back, this experience held some valuable lessons:

1. A qualified person should give instructions for the IDP and understand the difference between training and development.

2. The benefits of and next steps of an IDP should be addressed.

3. The IDP can be a useful tool or hold zero value for the individual and, therefore, the organization.

Organizations have to go beyond a "box checker" mentality. An IDP is a working document for *development*. If there is no organizational support for advanced training coupled with development opportunities for the employee after completing an IDP, why is the organization using it? When there is no value to an IDP, it becomes a waste of time and money.

I learned to manage my development during this time at the organization. I realized I had to approach my Director to get permission to attend opportunities that interested me. Through my efforts, I did get noticed for having a desire to expand my capabilities. Eventually, I was approached for additional learning [development] opportunities outside of my then-current job description.

The Learning Organization

The most confident organizations are those who tailor their development programs to the needs of their employees and spend the money it takes to make it happen.[68] Up and coming leaders will be more diverse in both thought and experience, working with gender, nationality, and age differences. Diverse environments have become the norm.

By developing strategies to embrace diversity, organizations become more culturally aware. Understanding cultural differences will allow organizations to develop and enhance their strategies to promote workplace competence.

Positioning career development programs as key strategies keep them from becoming an afterthought. Organizations that are learning engines develop their people with intention; to be better, stronger leaders. By creating a learning organization, the environment can further align and support individuals with knowledge, skills, and experiences. Leaders who seek to grow their leaders and followers allow them to have a greater knowledge base of differences in the workplace, and use them to their organizational advantage.

Training vs. Development

Development opportunities are not training modules on a computer. Although training is part of most organizations, the difference between training and development is often unclear. Research shows training does not have a lasting impact on the individual nor the organization.[69] Although you would probably tell me you have a training *and* development budget, and you attend training and development functions, do you know the difference?

Organizations that strive to be at the top of their game know successful outcomes are attained through a multi-faceted development practice.[70] Training and development is a strategic process. In a 2012 article in Forbes Magazine, Michael Myatt outlined the differences in training and development.[71] As you read the differences, the disparities become clearer. The article suggests training is concerned with best practices and development is about *next* practices. If a leader's focus is only on training, there will be a lack of development.

Here are some of Myatt's examples:

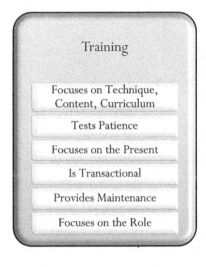
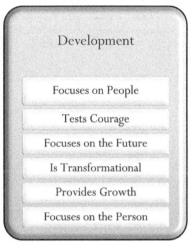

Training	Development
Focuses on Technique, Content, Curriculum	Focuses on People
Tests Patience	Tests Courage
Focuses on the Present	Focuses on the Future
Is Transactional	Is Transformational
Provides Maintenance	Provides Growth
Focuses on the Role	Focuses on the Person

To help paint a picture, think of the last *training* you went to. Was it a conference, or maybe a "box checker" class you needed to complete to keep your position or certification? Perhaps you were excited about the content from the conference or course and left with good intentions of implementing a new skill or idea? Three weeks go by, and you do absolutely nothing. Your good intention becomes just a faded memory. Does this sound familiar?

It's up to leaders to strategically create intentional opportunities for development and have accountability in place. Otherwise, your people are left with empty promises that are never acted upon.

Next practices consist of crafting a development and learning culture within the organization. This includes the leader's personal development. Senior leadership involvement and commitment are necessary to gain a strong development climate. Why? Because there is a link between formal human talent development [growth and performance] and the potential contribution [outputs and profitability]. When both are aligned, individuals and organizations reach a collective success.

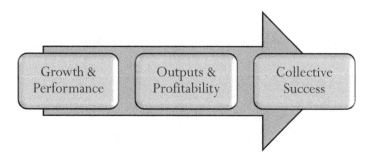

Leadership development programs must close the gap between what needs to be learned and the correct delivery method, noting the differences between business and organizational culture. This is accomplished through a combination of developmental assessments, personal reflection, and organizational performance criteria. Although HR assists in providing development opportunities for their people, the onus lies with the individual to accept the opportunity. And, in some cases, create those opportunities for themselves.

Myatt's suggestion for development is to exchange old school training for development activities like discipleship, mentoring, and coaching. Mentoring and discipleship have many similarities, yet, the differences are apparent: the mentor pours in, and the disciple becomes like the discipler.[72]

Although professional coaching is part of the helps profession, the practice is significantly different than both mentoring and discipleship. As a practice, professional coaching is a powerful way to strengthen organizational learning and performance at all levels.[73] Through establishing relationships, expanding self-reflection, and guiding development, professional coaching produces remarkable and measurable development results through improved effectiveness for the individual and organization. Learning is activated. This learning adds value to the person, but also adds value to their organization. When organizations develop their people, companies achieve shared value, rather than strictly shareholder value.

Developing The "Jagged Edge"

Do you realize how unique you are? There is no one quite like you. You may have similar characteristics or abilities as others, but no one in this world is *you*.

Everyone is born with talent. Fostering talent illuminates' purpose. Isn't everyone searching for meaning and purpose? Purpose is not pie in the sky talk. Along with talent, we are each born with and created for a purpose. Unfortunately, and for many, the busyness of the world keeps the answer to the million-dollar "what's my purpose" question at bay. When leaders take time to understand their own and others' talents, the answer will become more evident. Having awareness allows an opportunity to define and design around talent. A customized design approach leads to more effective individual development and a stronger organization.

Therefore, aligning development opportunities for the individual is crucial. As a leader, you and your staff require cultivating and continuous crafting. This means looking at and embracing the jagged edges (talent) of your people.

Think of a mosaic. The pattern of a mosaic comes from various shaped pieces of glass, clay, stone, or other material. At first sight, you may think the material the artist chooses could never be pieced together in an orderly fashion. However, when the artist strategically arranges the jagged edges, they become a collective, meaningful creation. The same is true of your people.

Your organization and teams are made up of jagged edges. Jagged edges are what makes each one of us unique. When you help individuals identify their jagged edges and purposely position them with others, you have the potential to magnify excellence within your organization. If leaders do not embrace and promote these edges, your pool of potential candidates will become stagnant. We'll dive deeper into jagged edge teams in a later chapter.

If embracing the concept of uniqueness and jagged edges sounds like it means change, you are correct. To foster the needed change, you may have to change your thinking. Think of it this way. It takes just as much energy to hire the right talent, offer effective development, or get everyone looking in the same direction as it does to supply your company with sub-par initiatives and deal with the fallout and cleanup.

Embracing the opportunity and encouraging others is part of the development process. When today's employees communicate what development opportunities matter to them, change occurs. However, it takes having a leader who hears their people. Sadly, when leaders overlook the unique make-up of each person, they find themselves with a workforce that is positioned to fail. An organization will not be positioned for sustainable success unless its *people* are. This means today's organizations, no matter what size, should increase their likelihood of success through development opportunities to attract, retain, and produce engaged leaders.

Engaging Your Talent

More times than not, I imagine you and your employees show up, put up, and give up time with family and friends to honor work commitments. People are searching for ways to bring meaning to their life, find purpose, and feel good about coming to work regardless of their pay grade. If the only satisfaction your employees receive from work is seeing their direct deposit at the end of the week, it's not enough. Earning that paycheck through using what some refer to as their God-given talent brings honor and satisfaction to your people.

The people who make up today's fast-paced organizations are often found working through lunch to meet deadlines and responding to emails outside of work. If they divide the hours worked into their salary, they might be working for less than minimum wage. What people have come to value in today's workplace is perceived differently based on what's important and relevant to the individual. What your employee values are the very things that keep them engaged.

As a leader, taking time to understand the power of engagement and managing your workforce takes getting to know your people and what motivates them. What drives your workforce is based on individual needs. I once thought to bring donuts in every Friday to let my people know they are appreciated was engagement. I was wrong. Bringing in donuts is a nice gesture, but the act did not speak to the heart and minds of my people or motivate them to work with excellence. It spoke to their sweet tooth. Although the act was thoughtful, it was far from developing human talent in my charge.

Employee engagement increases when you have boots on the ground. Therefore, it's necessary for leaders to recognize, listen to, and embrace their employee's needs. Leaders who do not commit to creating an engaged culture miss opportunities to become proficient in touching the hearts and minds of their people. This proficiency is demonstrated by knowing what matters to them. Furthermore, because of this neglect, the organization as a whole suffers. If you currently provide a cookie-cutter benefits package, it's time to innovate.

Engagement begins with understanding your people. This may look different based on generation, gender, or national origin. By knowing what questions to ask, listening to employee needs, and finding ways to fill the gap, employee development efforts are informed and can go a long way. When a well thought out engagement package is created during the recruitment and hiring stage, one that is meaningful to the employee, a win-win is generated for the individual and the organization.

The Experience

Deloitte's research discusses the importance of "employee experience." Many organizations do not view this experience as a priority. Every part of the organization contributes to and formulates the employee experience. This means a good experience for some may not be suitable for all. The impact of the experience is dependent upon the individual. Seeing your organization through the lens of the diverse workforce that you employ is vital for the health of your organization. Integrating national culture into your organizational design creates a more significant impact in the workplace.

I had the pleasure of meeting with a leader who works in the *Guest Experience* segment of a well-traveled Florida airport. Having traveled in and out of many airports, including the one she leads, it took her speaking three words, "airport" and "guest experience" for me to begin recalling my good and not so good guest experiences in airports. The experience this leader provides is not just to guests who are traveling. She provides a *guest experience* for her employees by way of development programs.

Take a moment and think of your people as guests. What experiences are you providing? When you think about those experiences, are they meaningful to the individual and the organization as a whole? The *positive* experience your people receive will increase engagement in the workplace.

Misconceptions of Employee Engagement

Employee engagement and creating a healthy employee experience are simple concepts, but are you activating an engaged workplace? You may think you engage your employees. The reality is you probably aren't, or not enough to make a difference. Remember, engagement has nothing to do with donuts!

Consider the following **misconceptions** of engagement in the workplace:

- If you pay more, you employ a more engaged workforce
- Fear promotes engagement
- An engaged employee stays engaged

Employee engagement has nothing to do with any of the above. You can't buy it, coerce it, or even keep it if engagement is not a priority for leadership.

Definitions of employee engagement include:

1. "a positive attitude held by the employee toward their organization and its values…. a two-way street between employer and employee,"[74]

2. "gets to the heart of what really matters to employees"[75]

In the State of the American Workplace report, Gallup® suggests engaged employees means employees are "involved in, enthusiastic about, and committed to their work and workplace." If you are or have ever been 'engaged' to a person before marriage, this may sound familiar. When an engagement ring is given and received, you are outwardly and *enthusiastically* committing to that person. Now think about your organization.

As a leader, are you outwardly and enthusiastically committed to your people? Likewise, are your people enthusiastically committed to your organization? Let's go one step further.

In that same report, Gallup® explains: "Employee engagement is not the same as engaging employees. Employee engagement is the **outcome** of actively engaging employees through a strategy that drives improved performance."[77]Re-read the sentence. It is important to understand the difference between employee engagement and engaging your employees.

According to Gallup® polls,[78]a staggering 87% of employees worldwide are not engaged! In the United States, this is a crisis. Of those polled, only 32% are engaged. This percentage is unacceptable, preventable, and cannot be fixed by engagement surveys like some may think. These surveys measure if the organization is providing its people with adequate support, rate their happiness, or satisfaction levels. Disappointingly, these surveys become "box checkers" when there is little or no follow-through on the part of the organization.[79]

> *Leaders who create an engaged culture become proficient in touching the hearts and minds of their people.*

When leaders develop and engage their people, they create innovative critical thinkers rather than mechanical, immobile employees. The impact is measurable.

Based on the Gallup® engagement research,[80] organizations with employee engagement scores in the top quartiles experienced:

> Lower absenteeism (41%)
> Lower turnover (59%)
> Lower shrinkage (28%)
> Fewer safety incidents (70%)
> Fewer quality checks and defects (40%)

Additionally, customer metrics (10%), productivity (17%), sales (20%), and profitability (21%) are higher! The outcomes of the research should, at the very least, pique your interest to learn more about employee engagement.

The Palace Group

Since 1980, The Palace Group, a South Florida multi-level senior living community, has provided excellence to its residents. With a mission statement that incorporates the Golden Rule, this organization is committed to exceeding expectations by demonstrating and delivering outstanding service.

I had the pleasure of meeting with Haim Dubitzky, Principal & Vice-President of Performance Excellence for The Palace Group. He is no stranger to the power of the Gallup® Employee Engagement Survey. The Palace Group has incorporated the Gallup® tool since 2015. The 2019 survey is the third under Mr. Dubitzky's leadership.

It's no surprise with a percentage of 95.6% of employees responding, people who work at The Palace Group take their engagement scores seriously. This mindset promotes accountability throughout the organization's hierarchy. Because of this dedication, The Palace Group is a two-time recipient of the Gallup® Great Workplace Award (2018, 2019). They join other workplaces such as Levi Strauss and Nationwide Insurance who are also recipients of this prestigious award.

According to Mr. Dubitzky, for organizations to meet with success, the process of engagement must be effectively managed. This management takes keeping his pulse on the data and recognizing when the data is off from inaccurate inputs.

When managed properly, valuable data emerges. This data gives the organization insight as they zero in on specifics. The Palace Group has used this data to generate truths in the workplace. For instance, the data uncovered employees who have family members working at the organization, are more engaged. Higher levels of engagement are also seen when employees have dual reports. Interestingly, the data identified those who commute the furthest to work are also more engaged.

The Palace Group effectively manages what was once a cause for concern. Mr. Dubitzky drills down and extracts information to combat disengagement in the workplace. Without data, the organization leaves engagement to chance.

Delivering Development Opportunities

When a continuous collaborative partnership between senior leaders and HR leaders is fully developed, successful employee engagement is found. This is a creative, on-going process. The process cannot be a once and done attempt to satisfy only the immediate needs of an organization. The process of fostering engagement is never-ending.

Further, this partnership also includes your employees. HR leaders must partner with lower level and supervisory leaders to identify and develop the talent pool through increasing skills, knowledge, and expanding their God-given capabilities. This is accomplished by providing learning opportunities to stretch the growing potential of your people.

There are several methods of delivery for human talent development.[81] Here are some examples:

Relationship Development: Mentors, peer-learning partners, social identity networks; professional coaching

Assignment Development: Job moves and rotations (even temporary), ex-pat positions, action learning projects (practical learning), leadership roles outside of work; professional coaching

Formal Feed-Forward Process Development: 360 degree-feedback, team peer-assessments, performance appraisals, professional coaching

Formal Program Development: Skill training plus implementation, university programs, personal growth programs, intensive feedback programs, professional coaching

Self-Development: Reading/writing articles, developing content, speaking at events, (town hall meetings, all staff meetings, or conferences), professional coaching

How many of the above development opportunities have you taken part in or provided for your people?

The Feedback Frenzy

The Millennial generation has spoken. Feedback is essential *and* expected. This generation desires to have more conversations around their performance in the workplace. If you're not a Millennial, lean in.

Feedback for this generation means frequent, quick, on the spot contact. The theory of promoting ongoing feedback is not so far-fetched. If you are seeking leadership excellence, this means bringing leaders into the feedback fold. Feedback is a mandatory practice.

When was the last time you asked for or gave feedback? I'm not talking about constructive criticism. Using the words constructive criticism is like scratching your nails on a chalkboard to many, including me. Putting the word constructive in front of a negative word does not make it any more positive. If you're shaking your head in disagreement, hear me out. What if we fed others forward?

When leaders feed-forward, having conversation meant to expand learning opportunities for motivating and encouraging, growth is generated. This means there is more than one person speaking. When feedback feeds forward, there is an opportunity to open the doors to better communication, deepen relationships, and increase engagement in the workplace and beyond.

It was evident from my interview with Mr. Dubitzky of The Palace Group, that the Gallup® tool has not just increased engagement, but has stretched the organization to innovate around feedback delivery. The organization developed and incorporates a robust feedback framework. This framework was birthed out of necessity. Constant feedback has become the expectation for those who work at The Palace Group. These feedback sessions are designed to feed their employees forward as management engages their employees in a safe environment.

As a leader, do you provide a safe environment for your people? Have you asked your people what learning opportunity excites them most?

When a continuous collaborative partnership between senior leaders and HR leaders is fully developed, successful employee engagement is found.

Have you asked for their input on a project? Or, ask for honest feedback to help your own leadership development? This feedback is gathered through formal assessments or informal conversations.

Much has been written on feedback.

Feedback is commonly used to *tell* people what they are doing wrong, instead of what they are doing right. This author believes leaders must do a better job developing meaningful communication processes to engage, empower, and grow their people. Leaders who choose excellence must change the way they design and present the feedback loop. Perhaps, ditch the word feedback altogether and replace the word and process with one that inspires rather than one that has become associated with fear and negativity.

The Disengaged Workplace

Disengagement occurs when organizations fail to provide adequate means to reach, encourage, and develop their people. Gallup® defines *not engaged* as employees who "are psychologically unattached to their work and company. Because their engagement needs are not being fully met, they're putting time — but not energy or passion — into their work." This research also notes that actively disengaged employees are found when "Employees aren't just unhappy at work — they are *resentful* that their needs aren't being met and are acting out their unhappiness. Every day, these workers potentially undermine what their engaged coworkers accomplish."[83]

According to the US Department of Labor, in 2012, disengagement cost the economy $300 billion annually.[84] More recent research determined employee disengagements costs US organizations $90 billion to $1.2 trillion per year.[85]These numbers alone should motivate you to take a look at your organization.

Disengagement also causes workers to enter a revolving organizational door on their quest to what's next. Research conducted by Harter and Adkins states 51% of the employees polled are either watching for openings or searching for new jobs. How engaged are your employees? Do they envision a future with your company? Are they enthusiastic?

Many years ago, I was sitting in a training session with some of my employees. The facilitator mentioned a statistic similar to the engagement research Gallup® provides. I looked around the table and thought, "who am I going to lose?" Instead, I should have been thinking, "*how can I prevent this?*"

As a leader, I knew I was chest-deep in the day-to-day operations of running the company. Although operations are an important part of keeping a business running, it takes *people* to sustain an organization. More could have been done to save a few great people from walking out the front door. My leadership could have been stronger during this period of time. I didn't know what I didn't know.

Gallup® argues, organizations that have an engaged workforce find their supervisors focus on strengths or positive characteristics (61%). When strengths are uncovered and mobilized, it bridges the gap between our worldly work and God's handiwork. Recognizing individual strengths becomes a breeding ground for increased engagement and collaborative relationships. Additionally, when the employee feels their manager is engaged, the employee is more engaged (59%).[86]

These percentages serve to inform leaders that we must do a better job of connecting with our employees and developing contributors to support the goals of the organization.

Collectively, your organization must work together to support individuals to move the leader's vision forward.

As a leader, your commitment to connecting relationally past your leadership team and deep into the heart of your organization will create a culture of engagement. However, that's not just the leader's responsibility; it's everyone's.

This collective force of responsibility takes collaborative and interconnected feedback. When feedback is offered and used to create meaning for employees, it drives engagement, creates motivation, and contributors are born. When your people are motivated, they will work tirelessly to bring the leader's vision to fruition. Why? Because deep down inside, they feel they matter. They become part of something bigger than themselves.

As you prepare to develop your people, look past the norm, under the exterior, and beyond what you think are their capabilities. Instead, reach into their masterful craftsmanship and seek to learn who they are as individuals and where their talents lie. Offer opportunities for them to *rise*, and become not just employees in the workplace, but contributors. When leaders help build contributors, the level of organizational success and excellence increases exponentially.

The Coaching Corner

1. How are your senior leaders and human resource leaders working together to obtain the very best talent?
2. What are some next steps to move this partnership forward?
3. How does your organization work toward illuminating and empowering individual "potential?"
4. What are some outdated talent management procedures you can toss in the garbage can?
5. What is your plan to develop yourself and/or your people by design and beyond the yearly "box-checker" requirements?
6. What types of training do you offer that can be bridged into development opportunities?
7. How do you know if your employees are engaged?

8. What development activities are creating growth for you as an individual and collectively for your organization?

9. What development activities are **not** creating growth for you as an individual and collectively for your organization? What is the next step?

10. Name three emerging leaders in your organization. How are you supporting their growth?

11. What development opportunities do senior leaders in your organization take part in on a regular basis?

Chapter 7

The Impact of Leader Succession Planning

"By failing to prepare, you are preparing to fail."
~Benjamin Franklin

In 2009, the Securities and Exchange Commission (SEC) identified the governance of successions as a "significant policy issue" that exceeds the day-to-day managing of staff. As the SEC defines it, succession is a Board of Directors (BOD) mandate.[87] However, it is the organization's Human Resource (HR) leaders who are required to optimize internal successions on a day-to-day basis. HR minimizes employment gaps by equipping leaders and establishing succession plans. Although the SEC published the ruling in 2009, the truth is, *most* board of directors do not understand nor participate in the day-to-day functions of the organization.

Moreover, in my observation as a past board member, many organizations do not have an active BOD, but a passive one. According to a 2015 Spencer Stuart Board Index report, over a third of the participating board members serve on three or more boards.[88]

Succession planning is complex. Having multiple commitments creates limitations in giving immediate issues precedence during the time succession planning requires.

HR leaders and transition teams make an impact on the future of the organization when they recognize the importance of implementing a succession plan.[89] The SEC does not define succession planning as an *operational* function but a strategic issue. This author would maintain succession planning is indeed a strategic issue and impacts overall operational functions.

A succession plan is a living document that should be developed, revisited, and revised as required. It is not a once a year event where IDP's of high potentials are brought before the Board of Directors for discussion. The succession plan is an actionable document that communicates a forward vision for the organization. Continuity is key to organizational success. This plan communicates to your staff that you are prepared for any bumps in the road that may happen along the way.

Therefore, the Board of Directors should invite and partner with HR leaders throughout the succession planning process. By doing so, transition teams are established, organizational needs assessed, and development opportunities aligned.

Why CEO Successions Fail

Succession planning, although critical to organizational sustainability, is often overlooked due to the complexity and difficulty it presents.[91] Board involvement increases the likelihood of a mandatory succession process. Leaving preparation to chance creates a lasting, negative impact on the organization.

Vital elements to succession planning include preparation, business planning, and planning for overlap with the involvement of the outgoing leader. In addition, continuous monitoring and evaluation are necessary.[92]Understanding these areas of the succession process gives a broader view of the need and increases the likelihood of a successful transition. According to research, CEO succession planning has the potential to fail if:

1. BOD involvement does not align the hiring criteria with the strategic needs of the organization
2. The BOD members are reluctant to approach the incumbent CEO
3. Attention is not given to other senior leaders and those below the CEO level[93]

There is importance in providing "identity, distinctive competence, and protection from anxiety" as part of succession planning.[94] When an organization does not have a succession plan in place, it may create unnecessary, negative disruption.

Although planning for vacancies is important at all levels, senior leadership succession planning is critical. Succession planning is instrumental in preparing the organization for the future. Additionally, succession planning alleviates the stress and anxiety of change, especially when change is unexpected.

Employee morale improves when an organization strategically manages succession planning and promotes from within. However, an internal candidate must be developed to rise into what will become a leadership vacancy successfully. It is not just employee morale that needs attention. It's all stakeholders, including investors.

It is up to HR leaders to serve, deliver, and ready their organizations to perform at the highest levels. The process of succession planning is more than filling vacancies, exercising appropriate risk management, and completing replacement planning. Succession planning is meant to be a stabilizing process.[95] Stabilization ensures effective performance by recognizing key people and positions that are strategically developed over time.

There were thirty-five S & P 500 CEO transitions in the first two quarters of 2017.[96] Four of the companies engaged an Interim CEO. Most transitions listed "retirement/stepped down"; however, five leaders "resigned under pressure" and one for "health" reasons. Only seven of the thirty-five incoming leaders have prior public CEO experience.

Female CEO Disproportion

In 2017, 7 females stepped into a CEO role. In 2018, there was one. In Q2 2019, 3 females took the helm. Based on these numbers, there's a lot of work to do. This work starts with you, the female leader. It's time to be confident and unapologetically RISE UP and *develop* your leadership. Be bold and courageous in your business ventures. It's your time to shine!

To the male leaders and BOD's, *you must be willing* to hire and develop the women in your charge. If you choose not to position the women in your organization for success, you will miss out on the wisdom and brilliance that women bring to the talent table.

Inattention to Succession Planning is Risky Business

Succession planning is complex. The complexity leaves some organizations feeling overwhelmed. However, the do *something* model of succession planning is better than the *do-nothing* model. In a fast-paced, ever-changing environment, it is negligent for leaders who practice excellence to ignore succession planning as a necessary tool for organizational sustainability.

Although succession planning should be in place for continuity of leadership and successful transitions, it lacks attention. This inattention may be one reason why succession planning is not a top priority among board members.

In a study of 124 board members:[97]

> 51% said they **do not** have an **emergency** succession plan in place, but know they should
>
> 45% said they **do not** have a **long-term** succession plan in place
>
> 52% agree the board will most likely hire an external candidate if they need to replace the current CEO in the next 12 months

Additionally, the derailment of successful succession planning is not unheard of. If the current CEO takes the position of being irreplaceable, she or he may feel it unwarranted to suitably train up a list of protégés.[98] This inattention to succession planning leads to an increased potential for derailment. Readying the outgoing leader during what may be an emotionally charged time is necessary for success.

Succession planning is not without risk. Strategically designing a process with best practices is necessary. Take note; risk and a failed attempt for sustainability will ensue when:[99]

- the process begins without first agreeing on the strategy for the company and the market factors that impact the senior leader role
- the process is started too late
- the involvement from the outgoing senior leader in choosing the successor hinders the process
- the unsuccessful internal candidates leave the organization
- the process is managed without professional advice from

consultants or a search firm
- the process becomes a distraction for the senior executive team
- the pool of candidates is only internal or only external
- the team has little experience with senior leadership successions
- the team lacks clarity between emergency and planned succession processes and actions
- the process is conducted without HR involvement
- the organization has successors who aren't ready
- the investors who are not on the board or selection team inhibit the process

Searching For Answers

A February 2017 Nationwide Insurance Company press release offers insight into succession planning and organizational readiness. In 2016, Nationwide hired Harris Polling to conduct succession-planning research. The research included 502 US-based business owners with less than 300 employees. Almost half of the participants said they do not have a succession plan in place. The reason? They do not believe it is necessary.[100]

2016 Harris Poll	Participants
Do not have a succession plan in place; it's not necessary.	47%
Ignoring; not wanting to give up one's life work.	14%
Not knowing when to create a plan.	11%
Not knowing who to work with.	11%
Not having time to develop a plan.	11%
Being overwhelmed with government regulations.	8%

The results in the Harris study are alarming but not surprising. Although the Harris poll focuses on the need for the financial and legal services Nationwide Insurance sells, it also shines a light on the lack of focus given to succession planning.

In a recent coaching session with a division leader, succession planning was explored. My client's organization has no formal plan in place. She candidly relayed, "I know that either by my own decision to leave or the company's decision to terminate my employment, I will eventually be replaced." When a leader experiences uncertainty for their future, it affects more than their work attitude and performance, it drips into other areas of their life.

The uncertainty my client was experiencing was alleviated when we explored her options. My client made an action plan. This action plan included advancing the conversation by meeting with decision-makers to pro-actively participate in her succession. This was a win for my client and a win for the organization.

Succession Planning By Generation

Our diverse workforce continues to grow, impacting today's organizations.[101]Leadership style, values, motivations, and commitment reflect generational differences.[102]

The Boomers are loyal, workaholics, competitive, embrace growth, and change;[103] are communicators, team players, and expect a traditional hierarchal structure.[104] Gen-Xers are independent, fun-loving, and self-reliant; [considered] less loyal; and prefer a balance of work and non-work life.[105]Lastly, the Millennials (Gen Y) are globally aware, a "connected" generation who are optimistic, accept diversity, are civic-minded, confident,[106] and challenge the status quo.[107] According to Gallup®, Millennials are the generation who are the most interested in opportunities for development.[108]

The Harris poll included each of these generations. As expected, Baby Boomers had a reduced representation in the poll as these business owners are slowly transitioning out of the workforce. The Harris poll also demonstrated that Boomers and Gen-Xers were equally lagging when it came to having a succession plan in place. Just 32% have a succession plan. Even Millennials, 61% of whom were found to have a succession plan in place, need to hang on to their egos. Sixty-one percent is far below the preparedness that is required in our fast-paced 21st-century organizations. Everyone has a lot of work to do.

Succession Plan by Generation

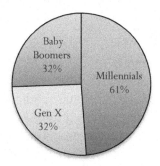

Boomers and Millennials see their roles through a different lens. Most Boomers gauge commitment with the amount of time they have stayed with their company. Millennials, on the other hand, are open to new ventures. This doesn't necessarily mean they are any less committed than Boomers. However, preparing for a departure may be more likely in the short term. Millennials are looking to work for an organization that aligns with what's important to them, including benefits and perks that support flexibility, family, and development.[109]

Baby Boomers need to have their succession plans firmly developed and readied throughout their organizations. Why? Because the Baby Boomers are the next generation to exit the workplace entirely. Even more importantly, the knowledge gained over the years must be passed on to younger generational leaders. The workplace often disregards the intellectual component and knowledge management of seasoned workers, and the wisdom that their longevity affords.

In contrast to the Harris poll, research gathered from Q1 and Q2 of 2017 S & P CEO successions listed earlier; twenty-two were a "planned succession." However, to what extent of planning is unclear. Nine of the thirty-five CEO successions did not indicate whether or not the succession was planned. Unplanned successions were for *health reasons*, *resigned under pressure*, or *retired/stepped down*.

Planned	Yes	N/A	No
Transition?	22	9	4

Strategy is a large part of an executive's position within an organization. As addressed at the beginning of the chapter, the SEC has identified succession planning as a necessary strategy. In 2016, the SEC proposed requirements of having business continuity and transition plans in place to lessen the burden or impact on clients,[110] which has had mixed reviews.[111]Some companies feel it is an unnecessary requirement and has already been addressed sufficiently.

Regardless of the size of an organization, profit or non-profit status, developing a succession plan makes good business sense. Succession planning looks at the past, identifies patterns that help bridge the gap, and anticipate future outcomes.[112]Bridging the leadership gap and anticipating results takes time and preparation.

When life happens, there will either be a plan or not. A large corporation without a plan may be in for a rocky ride. For a small business, if no one comes to the helm to lead, the business may be sold to pay off its debt, or the doors may close for good. In either case, it's about survival. Survival takes planning.

What Happens When No One's In Charge?

Life happens, and it's not always convenient. Having a catastrophic event impact the workplace may bring clarity to answering the "who" and "how" questions: *Who is in charge, and how do we move forward?* Let's use the example of the well-known Silicon Valley company that employed 550 people.[113]

The tragic death of Survey Monkey CEO David Goldberg was a disrupter in the Survey Monkey world. Mr. Goldberg was a 47-year-old Gen-Xer who died suddenly while on vacation with family and friends in Mexico. This CEO had been at the helm of Survey Monkey for six years. Based on reports, his unexpected passing left the company without a named replacement.[114] Survey Monkey's board interviewed 75 candidates before naming Zander Lurie as the temporary executive in charge. Three months after Goldberg's death,

Hewlett-Packard's COO Bill Veghte was hired as the Survey Monkey CEO.[115]   However, in January 2016, just six months after his appointment as CEO, Lurie replaced Veghte, citing differences in strategic direction.[116]

Although Bill Veghte continues to serve Survey Monkey as a board member,[117] his *fit* as CEO did not align with the future of the company. Lack of alignment is a clear demonstration of the need to develop a succession plan that identifies high potentials and equips them for future positions.

Sigma-Aldrich Corp was in a similar situation as Survey Monkey in November of 2010.[118]Their CEO, Jai P. Nagarkatti, died unexpectedly at the age of 63.[119] The board of directors acted quickly, announcing both Mr. Nagarkatti's death and his replacement with Rakesh Sachdev the following day. Previously, Mr. Sachdev served as the CFO and Senior Vice President of International Affairs.[120] Because of the organization's well-defined succession plan, this succession was quickly managed. In the case of Mr. Nagarkatti, succession planning development and implementation transformed the occurrence of the unimaginable into a well-defined and managed transition.

> *Bridging the leadership gap and anticipating results takes time and preparation.*

Although leadership is vital, leaders *are* replaceable. The reason to actively work a succession plan is far more important than the reason behind the replacement. Leaders who practice excellence must seek wisdom and know "when to say when." This concept is difficult for some leaders to grasp.

The act of succession planning development and implementation takes courage, humility, and wisdom. These virtues are also needed by the individuals involved in stepping in, out, or down from a role within a succession plan. There is a season for every activity and every leader.

Do you remember the song, *Turn, Turn, Turn* by the Byrds? The lyrics of this number one Billboard hit of 1965 are taken almost verbatim from a great book of wisdom, Ecclesiastes. Ecclesiastes Chapter 3 vv. 1-8 communicates [in a sense] it's okay for each of us to number our days. Everything and everyone has an expiration date.

Leaders may need to be prompted about the importance of

succession planning, especially when it comes to their successor. If the *nothing's ever going to happen to me* thinking is present, you are setting yourself and those in your organization up for failure.

Survey Monkey should serve as an eye-opening example. Any change is difficult, but without strong leadership and a robust succession plan, when a vacancy is unexpected, it produces unnecessary stress and anxiety for the entire organization. The sooner leaders come to terms with this thinking, the better prepared your organization will be.

Succession Planning and the 21st Century

When done right, a succession plan provides adequate bench strength for both planned and unplanned vacancies.[121] It is negligent to overlook the talent that resides inside and underneath the C-Suite. The benefits of the succession plan increase when a plan is built on trends that correlate with purposeful organizational development opportunities.[122] This means leaving bias at the door and linking employee ability to business objectives to fill a known or potential gap with the appropriately developed people. When an organization leverages the links, succession planning can flow from what is needed, to whom, and how.

Succession planning is just that, planning for one person to succeed another. It is not replacement planning. Leaders are charged to do more than name a replacement; *they must develop them.*

There is a strategic approach from inception to completion to develop for a future need. This is long-range planning and design. There is a myriad of possible design options when developing a succession plan. The design of a succession plan may look different depending on the vacancy, internal high potential readiness, and the allotted time that has been established to complete the process.

> *When senior leaders are only focused on extinguishing fires, they remain in a constant state of living from moment to moment rather than anticipating the future needs of the organization.*

Wisdom & Direction

Survey Monkey did not have a plan in place for its CEO vacancy. Conversely, Sigma-Aldrich Corp had a well-defined plan.

As organizations look to critical trends and embrace a futuristic approach to hiring and retention, they create a competitive advantage. It takes opening hearts and minds to identify promptings for wisdom and direction.

It is up to all leaders to strategically partner with HR management to discuss the vision of the organization and what talent *fits into* that future. Through the leader's vision, HR departments serve their organization by developing individuals and creating succession plans that embrace the living values and ethics the organization has adopted.

The Coaching Corner

1. How can succession planning prepare your organization for the future?
2. Who manages succession planning in your organization? How often are the plans revisited?
3. If there is no succession plan, what is one step you can take to begin to set a strategy in motion?
4. If the CEO or another senior leader of your organization did not return tomorrow, name the person who would replace her or him. What development opportunities might this person benefit from?
5. Who is your best-fit pick if you did not return to your position tomorrow? On a scale of 1-10 [1 low], how prepared is your best-fit pick to step into your role?
6. Which succession narrative impacted you most? Why?
7. What development opportunities are currently available to prepare internal candidates for the next succession?

Chapter 8

Leading Strategy

"Hope is not a strategy"
~Vince Lombardi

What comes to mind when you think of strategy? Do you think of a blueprint, a roadmap, a plan, or maybe even a procedure? All of these references are correct. However, we are going to look at strategy with new eyes; as a *unifying process* where strategic teams prioritize and focus on managing the implementation process.[123]

Strategy brings together individual thoughts, ideas, and potential pathways while identifying values, beliefs, and expectations. To develop strategy, an organization must look both internally and externally or as Simoneaux and Stroud[124]suggest, looking in the mirror and out the door. Leaders cannot develop a strategy without understanding the vision or needs or the organization. Strategic leaders realize completing short-term objectives is a constant long-term journey. Strategy encompasses near and long-term goals.

Strategy is also about change. It is the progression of change that continually builds and creates a long-term, impactful strategic competitive advantage for an organization. Change is often difficult for organizations to work through unless they have a plan that links vision to action. Without a plan, there are no results to measure. As many would think, strategy is not always clear and well-defined. It does, however, take critical elements for leaders to be able to think, act, and influence towards reaching a *sustainable* competitive advantage.[125]

Regardless of the objective, strategic planning and execution are not accomplished by a lone leader. Each initiative, program, project, or endeavor, must align with a competent team [or teams] who overcome challenges, have identified measurable markers, and who celebrate successes. Strategy reveals wisdom. That wisdom is generated through a team who thinks inside and outside the box. They imagine and discuss the 'what ifs.' The outcomes of this discussion drives the organization towards obtaining a sustainable competitive advantage in the marketplace.

Why Is Strategy Important?

Some may say strategy is only about outcomes, but it is more than that. Strategy is about *people creating outcomes* and generating broader thinking. When leaders broaden their thinking, there is an opportunity to create. Creating a way forward that first understands the organizational make-up is necessary.

Uncovering organizational culture isn't rocket science. The culture of your organization can be found by asking a simple question, "how do we do things around here?" Valuable insight is gained by asking this question. Organizations should not discount the values the culture accepts and believes as truth.

Creating A Strategic Environment

Leadership is a critical component of change efforts. The leader's alignment of skills and abilities are critical to the mission and vision of the organization. A strategic leader paints a picture of the organization's future for their people.

When an organization is ready to strategize and put the vision into action, there is a need for unification. Unification means people who are 100 percent engaged, committed and invested in the process. Managing the environment and the process streamlines the approach.

The process of strategic management is about agreeing where to focus.[126] Don't be surprised if each team member views this focus differently. The challenge is to go beyond one's self and decipher, where the group's energy and effort should be placed. The group must engage in a unification framework that provides motivation, outlines a format where everyone is treated with respect, and differences are accepted and appreciated. In addition, expectations must be set early

106

and clearly stated. This aids commitment and cohesion. However, as stated in an earlier chapter, the example the leader provides will dictate how and what your team produces.

The commitment of the group will reflect the investment the leader portrays to the group. Therefore, the leader must exemplify and encourage a collaborative effort and provide for an active learning environment.

The goal is to gain a successful strategy that makes sense to the team. This goal must be relevant to the organizational future. This successful outcome comes as team members identify strategic intent, learn to lose self-interest, and find themselves committed to being focused on the big picture, linking vision to action.[127] Being part of a strategic team creates an engine that advances learning individually and collectively.

The Learning Engine

Becoming a learning engine equips an organization to continually strive to embrace opportunities through an ongoing state of formulation, implementation, reassessment, and revision.[128] Teams need a road map, one that asks relevant questions and uncovers what's necessary to learn. Checking the boxes to the following five key elements supports this phase:

Teams must:

- make sense out of the organizational environment by clarifying vision, mission, and core values
- understand where they need to go and why
- have clear priorities, and reasonable objectives set, relayed, and focused upon
- progress measurements are crafted and reassessed at each new level of performance

The learning cycle filters through each stage and begins again.

Each of the above areas requires a leader who sets the vision. It also requires a team that aligns strategy with the leader's vision. We'll dive into *strategically* assembling teams in a later chapter.

Having the ability to link *thought to action* may be easy for a leader. However, not all actions are strategic, and not all strategies will be carried out as planned.[129] An effective leader understands key developmental tasks that require necessary action. Through strategic thinking, strategic acting and influence occurs.

Long and short-term strategies are imperative for success. As a strategic leader, speaking to the emotional and creative side of your people is necessary. This action generates motivation. Motivation takes the organization from learning 'how to get there, through the journey, and checks progress along the way.' The strategic leader does not lose focus during the learning process but is passionately committed to the strategy.

Overcoming Challenges

Leaders must determine where and with *whom* to focus their efforts to move strategy forward. Leaders often face environmental challenges, which include stakeholders, regulatory requirements, and human resources. Each offer unique circumstances.

> *Through strategic thinking, strategic acting and influence occurs.*

Stakeholders

Although stakeholders change, it is up to leadership to continue to strive to build identity and commitment through adhering to the organizational mission, and abiding by all regulatory standards. Stakeholders are affected by each of these. Stakeholder influence can negatively impact the organization.[130] Stakeholders hurt strategy by unknowingly [and sometimes knowingly] sabotaging efforts due to self-interest.

Aligning the Organization

Understanding issues is a springboard towards the end goal, but leaders and managers must align, and create a trickle-down effect within. Research indicates groups who lack cohesion work against each other while cohesive groups are more likely to accomplish group goals.[131] Furthermore, conflict may occur depending on the values and worldview that each stakeholder holds.

Organizational mission, vision, and code of conduct must be aligned, understood, have meaning, and be relevant. Having a mission and vision statement etc. for some, is nothing more than a "box-checker" item. How often are the words re-visited, and the ultimate question asked, "Is this still relevant?" This question keeps alignment at the forefront.

Commitment

Commitment is obtained by building an engagement framework to include: participation, leadership behavior, and communication.[132] Individuals typically desire a positive outcome or strategy that leans toward their personal interests. It is up to leadership to harness and constrain self-interested parties to maximize strategic efforts for the organization as a whole.

Lack of Focus

Organizations that lack focus, avoid difficult choices, and refuse to discriminate fall into the *kitchen-sink strategy* category.[133] This strategy leads to being overcommitted and pressed for time. When leaders throw the kitchen sink strategy into the mix, expect the process to be messy. Leaning in on team members who keep the team out of the kitchen is beneficial.

Success on Purpose

It is attention that fosters strategic competency improvement.[134] Uncovering the competencies that need improvement should be addressed and monitored. When improvements are made, the individual leader grows. Growth offers a residual impact on the team as well as the organization.

A leader and their organization stay on task by checking metrics that are based on the organization's strategic drivers. Contracting a "knowledge provider" or having one on staff for reviewing progress is beneficial. Performance measures are indicators, and those indicators must have accountability attached to them. Error detection and correction is part of organizational learning.[135] With the help of a consultant and a leadership coach who works with teams, your organization will generate a higher return for the investment you've made to your strategy.

What a company looks like in 5 years will be different than at 20 years. This difference will dictate how the organization is going to get to where they would like to go. By developing strategic competencies, leadership and their organizations are better positioned for developing, planning, and implementing successful strategies that lead to a sustained competitive advantage.

Leaders and teams must keep their pulse on the project and steer away from conflict, inaction, and self-serving practices. Leveraging a diverse team that commits to unity, the greater good, effectively communicates, and aligns toward a shared vision is essential.

The strategic leader does not lose focus during the learning process, but is passionately committed to the strategy.

The Coaching Corner

1. How do you define strategy?
2. When did your team experience success implementing strategy? What made it successful?
3. When did you meet with a failed outcome?
4. What could have been done to prevent failure?
5. What are the five key elements to generating an ongoing state of formulation, implementation, reassessment, and revision?
6. What is a kitchen sink strategy? How can this type of strategy hinder progress?
7. What and who makes strategy successful?

Chapter 9

The Value of Strategic Competencies

*"So often people are working hard at the wrong thing.
Working on the right thing is probably more
important than working hard."*
~Caterina Fake

There are tremendous benefits to crafting a culture to create a meaningful, strategic contribution to the organization. Competitive advantage comes as organizations seek to add value to their current strategies and develop their employees by design.

To establish a strong, meaningful culture, formal and informal processes, values, traditions, and expectations must be aligned. This alignment will help create a culture that is capable of experiencing long-lasting transformational change for the individual and the organization. Still, in today's fast-paced, continually changing world, designing a successful strategy may seem like a daunting task for most strategic teams.[136]Focusing on key questions links thought to action.

Partnering For The Future

The partnership of senior leaders and strategic teams will benefit from a practitioner who works with teams to guide the organization's learning process. This process begins with partnering and equipping your strategic team.

Without changed thinking, nothing will change. Therefore, strategic change requires strategic thinking that entails hard [analytical] and soft [quantitative] skills as shown below:[137]

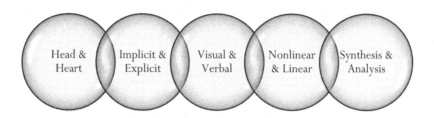

As leaders think strategically, they must engage hard and soft skills. This combination of skills is difficult for some leadership teams to grasp.

Leaders must develop insight and discernment as "the realities of the world bring new realities to followers, and they begin to look at problem-solving from new angles."[138]

Earlier, we defined strategic thinking as seeing.

To think strategically requires *"seeing ahead and behind, seeing above and below, seeing beside and beyond, and seeing it through."*[139] If leaders are to see the organization and themselves, clearly, they must leave no stone unturned.

Strategy is about broader thinking and people creating outcomes. Strategy takes uncovering 'what ifs,' and gaining wisdom from the team. Are you surprised to learn most leaders do not have well-developed thinking competencies?[140]

For strategies to be successful, organizations must continually ask questions internally and externally. Leaders who strive to embrace strategic change, such as executing a strategic initiative, must adopt an ongoing state of formulation, implementation, assessment, and revision.[141] But first, they must peel back the onion on their organization and see what the organization is comprised of.

As a practitioner of leadership development, I help strategic organizational processes. Through on-going coaching, senior leaders learn to increase their strategic thinking competencies, define clear objectives, and a way forward.

A strategic leader is willing to invest. This investment takes time and effort to see beyond today and envisions the organization of the future with the help of establishing partnerships.

When aligning any strategy into organizational culture, internal and external challenges must first be identified. Organizations have to look in the mirror (internal) and out the door (external).[142] Threats and opportunities are often present in the external environment.[143] Strategic thinking competencies and questions to ask include:

- Scanning: What can we become?
- Visioning: Where do we need to go?
- Re-Framing: How can we see things differently?
- Making Common Sense: What is our shared understanding of the organization?
- Systems Thinking: What complexities are underneath the Big Picture?

Let's take a look at how challenges of internal and external alignment played out for a well-known company, Johnsonville Sausage.

Johnsonville Sausage

Ralph Stayer, owner of Johnsonville Sausage, realized his current workplace strategy was not effective. His company wasn't losing revenue, but there was an evident problem. Stayer's people were not engaged and Johnsonville had quality control issues. Mr. Stayer created a management style that "kept people from assuming responsibility."[146] His desire to have a more engaged workplace began by looking at how he was running things.

As the senior leader of his company, *he* was the problem! Instead of the employees being contributors, Mr. Stayer created a culture where he fostered an expectation of his people to be less than capable. Mr. Stayer's failure to effectively manage revealed his limitations. This failure to manage effectively, coupled with tight control as a leader, resulted in a misalignment of people and processes.

Mr. Stayer engaged his people in a change process. Internal teams were formed to research organizational processes, including quality control. They looked at external factors, examining how their retailers were handling Johnsonville products. After the team learned packaging issues shortened the shelf life of their product, they found solutions for quality control. Mr. Stayer learned his people were more than capable; they just needed *permission* to demonstrate their capabilities.

Stayer realized he alone could not manage his people. He needed people strategies that allowed the right people to participate and invest in the company to create a prosperous future.

Uncovering the Future

How do you scan, identify, and secure the future of your organization? If you are unable to answer this question, the time is now to begin.

Successful organizations track the future and decipher what are threats and what could be an opportunity for growth. They implement approaches from learned or sometimes failed strategies as a way to re-define, update, and refine their activities.[147] The first requirement is to understand the conditions of the organization's effectiveness, adapt to those conditions, and navigate through the opportunities that are available for making strategy a learning process. Ralph Stayer did just that as he moved his company [and his thinking] from mismanaged quality control measures to crafting a strategy for change.

Tracking the Future

In the 21st century, it is up to all levels of the organizational strategic team to give insight and prepare for what is to come.[148] Foresight is needed to develop strategies. Why? Because we do not have prophetic knowledge. For leaders, the ability to cast a vision based on what is known and what is to come, even if uncertain, remains a critical component of designing today's organizations. Designing the future by creating visionary strategies is a learned process.

The learning process seeks to understand both internal and external environments. Due to growth on a global level, diverse environments are the norm. Human resource executives are expected to be fully aware of changes in population, innovation, and the competitive nature of future talent, recruitment, and retention. As organizations become aware of their future and choose efforts that align with their desired future, change will follow. Organizations position themselves toward the future by seeking to understand where innovation fits with strategy.[149] That strategy must include current and future hires.

As the world changes in the name of innovation, individuals, and organizations alike must be ready for the future world, yet be mindful that assumptions, trends, and human action alter the course outcome. Scanning the environment assists with seeing the future and guiding results.

Scanning creates awareness for leaders and strategic teams.

Here are a few examples of "creating awareness" questions strategic teams must answer when looking to define their way for development programs [but can be used with any strategic initiative]:

1. What has changed in our industry?
2. What do our current development programs look like?
3. Do our development programs ready and maximize the potential of our people and align with future organizational needs? How do we know?
4. Are we seeking to employ anyone, or are we looking to onboard and retain contributors for our organization?
5. Are we hiring for innovation using backward thinking/hiring?
6. Besides our people, what are our competitive advantages?
7. What are the strengths, weaknesses, opportunities, and threats for implementing a development [or other strategic] initiative?

Having answers to questions like these create awareness and determining the state of the current organization as a whole. Attention and monitoring may be needed.

Focusing on the Future

Today's vision must move toward what trends indicate. Leaders must understand how to cultivate the future based on areas of change. Hiring managers need direction when assessing who to hire. Opinions are often based on a lack of data. Relying on instincts often presents bias[150] and blind spots.

> As the world changes in the name of innovation, individuals and organizations must be ready for the future world.

In a global age, diversity in the workplace means gender, ethnic, generational, and faith differences are areas to consider in the future fit organization. The key to cultural renewal is releasing human potential.[151] With human resource development, the future vision of the organization, along with the identification of future trends, reveals what skills and abilities the future employee must demonstrate to move the company forward.[152]

The commitment of the strategic team for any change effort will reflect the investment the leader portrays to the group. Therefore, the leader must exemplify and encourage a collaborative effort amongst the team and provide an active learning environment.

Examples of "future-focused" questions strategic teams must answer are as follows:

1. What is our vision, mission, and what are our core values?
2. How do our vision, mission, and values align with who we are as an organization?
3. How do they align with our strategic initiative?
4. What adjustments have to be made to get us where we want to go?
5. How do our current development opportunities account for diversity and globalization?
6. What impact can a coaching initiative have on our organization?
7. If we stop limiting our organization, what can we become?
8. What challenges might be ahead? How do we confront these?

Activating the Future

There must be a strategic bridge between vision and action. Having the ability to link thought to action may or may not be easy for a leader. Not all actions are strategic, and not all strategies will be carried out as planned.[153]

The six general competencies of strategic acting include:[154]

1. Setting clear priorities
2. Creating conditions for others' effectiveness
3. Making strategy a learning process
4. Acting decisively in the face of uncertainty
5. Acting with short and long-term goals in mind
6. Having courageous convictions

Leaders must go beyond self-focus and decipher, where the strategic team's energy and effort are to be placed. The goal is to gain a successful strategy that makes sense to the strategic team in relation to their organizational future. This successful outcome occurs or develops as the strategic team members learn to lose self-interest and find themselves committed to focusing on the big picture. The big picture links vision to action.[155]

Examples of "linking" questions strategic teams must answer:
1. What is our priority?
2. Who do we need to help us "get there?"
3. What resources are available?
4. Who will fund the effort?
5. What might we have to give up or reduce to gain this strategic initiative?
6. How do we share what we've learned with our organization?

An effective leader understands key developmental tasks take necessary action. It is first through strategic thinking that strategic acting and influence can occur, with conviction.

> *Not all actions are strategic, and not all strategies will be carried out as planned.*

Strategic convictions blend "thinking and emotion, information and intention, anticipation and aspiration."[156]

Measuring Progress

All strategic initiatives must be measured and reassessed at each new level of performance. Analysis of measurements and assessments create a continuous learning cycle. This learning cycle will result in refinements to the process that is currently in place.

As strategy unfolds, understanding patterns and causal relationships are crucial. Performance measures are indicators, and those indicators must have accountability attached to them. Error detection and correction is part of organizational learning.[157]

Barriers to Overcome

Developing organizations that tackle initiatives stretching past social, economic, political, and cultural boundaries do not do so without challenges. Diversity is a breeding ground for disagreements, where values become questioned or challenged, and cultural assumptions are misleading.[158]A strong leader must create intentional, respectful bridges within the strategic team, but those bridges must also reach into the organization.[159]Strategic teams must learn to be interconnected and collaborative rather than segregated.

Likewise, the strategic team is not made up of one lone member. Instead, a strategic team is comprised of many members who are uniquely designed and gifted with distinct strengths. When strategic teams realize the value that interconnectedness brings to the team dynamic and organizational initiative, it provides depth and breadth. This depth and breadth help teams when barriers arise.

Strategic teams must overcome barriers in communication, innovation antibodies, climate, readiness, and commitment.

Communication

Many times, communication is a barrier to a successful strategic initiative. Strategic teams may communicate differently based on their area of expertise.[160]A CPA may communicate and want to initiate priorities based on the needs of their division. This communication may look very different than someone at the table from HR. If norms are not in place to provide for open and honest communication, team members may be reluctant to challenge leadership or each other. This will lead to a failed strategy.

Strategic teams are developed to impart strategic implications to an assigned area of an organization, and each member must understand their own and their team members' goals and roles concerning the strategy. Team function may be weak when members feel they are not adding value to the process, interpretation differs, or information sharing is delivered differently based on national culture.[161]

Innovation Antibodies

As strategic teams move toward an initiative, they must continually be aware of how change affects the organization. In every organization, there are "innovation antibodies." These antibodies are the naysayers. They see only failure and take a negative stance. Innovation antibodies are what Dr. Gary Oster calls, "dangerous idea wreckers." Oster further suggests the more radical the innovation effort, the more strongly innovation antibodies will attempt to interrupt the initiative.[162]

Innovation antibodies have an adverse effect on the strength of a proposed change initiative. Top executives may be the very source of diminishing that strength.[163] The key to scaling innovative change is for the strategic team to have senior leader buy-in.[164]

To combat innovation antibodies, strategic teams must demonstrate trust, communication, and transparency. Clarifying how change can assist the organization will neutralize innovation antibodies. Starting an initiative with small, rapid trials that are not costly can help manage increasing innovation antibodies along with small, consistent wins.[165]

Climate

A strategic team lends itself to multiple individual perspectives, experiences, and data that come together as teams assemble, and work as a unit.[166] Organizational cultural norms, behavior, values, customs, and attitudes are established over time within organizations. Climate is an indication of the internal environment based on the team member or on a wider scale, the team member's perception within the organization. Climate is about the environment as much as the individual or team experience.[167]

The temperature of a strategic team influences behavior.[168] It is likely an uncertain climate will include heightened tension, which leads to increased conflict, and lowered trust and morale. Tension raises the temperature for the strategic team.

Strategic teams maintain a good working climate when commitment and actions align with goals. Further, shared values and a mutual emotional climate will influence the effectiveness and efficiency of the team.[169] This influence will help deflect resistance to change.

Leadership regulates the temperature of the organizational climate as they invite others into the strategic process. The goal is to develop or define a successful strategy that makes sense to the strategic team in relation to their organizational future. This successful outcome is attained when team members unify and mature as a strategic team.

Organizational & Employee Readiness

Readiness is an important topic for the strategic team to address. Unless the organization is fully willing and able to commit and implement strategy, it will meet with failure. It is ultimately up to decision-makers to advance an initiative.

In addition to the decision-makers being ready to make a commitment to an initiative, there must also be team readiness. Individual readiness is inherent to successful organizational change implementation, which includes a readiness of both state (the belief change is needed) and process (recognizing the benefit and need).[170] Employees within the organization must be ready for the change process as resistance to change may occur without proper preparation.

Strategic teams must create buy-in for employees. A foundation of trust that is mutually shared positively impacts the influencing process and strategic outcome.[171] Although employees change, it is up to members of the strategic team to continue to strive to build identity and commitment to reducing ambiguity. Educating the organization is a key element. Change within an organization and individually is more likely if the employee sees the opportunity of an initiative as growth and development, and the change is aligned with their values.[172]

Commitment

Strategy is about defining objectives, understanding purpose, and building support based on key questions or issues.[173] When a leader is inconsistent or neglects to focus on the strategy, confusion, and mixed signals occur. This confusion limits what can be.

Managers, groups, and individuals typically desire a positive outcome or strategy leaning toward their personal interests. It is up to the strategic team to harness and constrain self-interested parties to maximize commitment across the organization as a whole.

Commitment is obtained by building an engagement framework to include participation, leadership behavior, and communication.[174] In an earlier chapter, you learned the process of strategic management is not just about the outcome but about *people* creating outcomes. In order for people to create outcomes, there needs to be involvement and participation.

Participation during the strategic process will unveil fresh and innovative thinking. Without changed thinking, nothing can change. The goal is to gain a successful strategy that makes sense to the group in relation to their organization's future. The successful outcome comes as group members lose self-interest and find themselves committed to being 100% focused on the big picture, linking vision to action.[175]

The Coaching Corner

1. What thinking competencies might you need to develop more fully?
2. How do you track, activate, and focus on the future of your organization? Is your future left to chance (default), or is it by design?
3. What measurements assist in your strategic endeavors?
4. How do your employees demonstrate they trust the strategic team to act on their behalf?
5. What barriers might hinder a strategic initiative in your organization?
6. How can you overcome these potential barriers?
7. How does your organization deal with innovation antibodies?
8. When might innovation antibodies help a strategic initiative?
9. What is the climate like in your organization, division, or department?
10. How do you ready your people for change? Does it work? Why or why not?
11. On a scale of 1-10 (1 low-10 high), how committed are your teams toward goal achievement? If your team is not at a 10, what is one action step that will bring the team closer to a ten?

Chapter 10

Building Strategic Teams

"Efforts and courage are not enough without purpose and direction."
~John f. Kennedy

Anyone can build a team, but not every team will be a well-oiled machine. High-performance teams have similar characteristics. They have a common purpose, establish trust, stay connected, communicate [often], collaborate, exhibit emotional and strengths intelligence, and celebrate their successes. Implementing an effective strategy takes building a strong team of internal individuals who work as partners to assess needs and find strategic solutions.[176]

Teams often assemble quickly regardless of country or time zone. Teams are expected to engage, strategize, and meet the goal at hand in a seamless fashion. These diverse, innovative teams have proven there is power behind strategically building teams for strength. When I am hired to design, build and/or support a team, leveraging strengths is a sure way to meet with success.

Going From "Me" To We

How do you assemble your team members? Do you design for success or by erroneous selections?

A strategic team operates in the state of being one body with many members, each working together. Togetherness begins with a clear, compelling, common purpose. Cohesive teams are more likely to accomplish group goals and feel a sense of belonging. However, teams who lack cohesion work against each other.[177]Cohesion is gained through trust. It's important to remember, team conversations are not a monologue, but a dialogue. When teams trust each other, it ignites this dialogue. It also generates spontaneity and unstoppable progress.[178] These demonstrations assert synergistic design.

By design, placing the right people in the right positions with the right talent and skills are essential for success. However, optimal coordination efforts also include relaying information through communication strategies across channels.

Communication throughout the strategic initiative creates awareness and alleviates ambiguity within the organization. By choosing to engage in cooperative efforts, the strategic team will transfer this cooperation to the overall organization. The outcome creates a common purpose and produces transparency, stability, and predictability.[179]

Misalignments of people equal low performance for the organization. Therefore, crafting alignment begins in first discovering the jagged edge.

The Jagged Edge

It has been said, well-roundedness breeds mediocrity. Do you want to be a mediocre leader or team member? If the answer is no, I ask that you entertain the jagged edge theory. We are not created well rounded, but have purposely crafted jagged edges. These edges are unique to each individual and not meant to be smoothed away. These jagged edges become a foundational springboard to advance our strengths.[180]

In Chapter 6, you learned jagged edges are compared to a beautiful mosaic. The pattern of a mosaic is created from various shaped pieces of glass, clay, stone, or other material. At first sight, you may think the material the artist chooses could never be pieced together in an orderly fashion. However, when the artist strategically arranges the jagged edges, they become a collective, meaningful creation. The same is true of your people.

> *If leaders do not promote "edginess" the team will be mediocre.*

Your organization and teams are not made up of perfect people. If you are looking for perfection, you will end up disappointed. No one can measure-up to something unattainable. We aren't designed to be perfect. Instead, we are designed with and for a purpose. That purpose includes other people.

Building strategic teams by embracing uniqueness generates excellence. Your team is comprised of unique individuals. Therefore, there is value in deliberately choosing individuals who have complementing jagged edges to comprise a team.[181] Jagged edges are what makes each one of us unique. When leaders help individuals identify their jagged edge and purposely orchestrate them into position, you have the potential to magnify excellence within your organization. If leaders do not promote "edginess" your team will be mediocre.

Finding Your Edge

As a Gallup® Certified Strengths Coach, this author posits the use of CliftonStrengths® to identify jagged edges and complementary offerings in building a strategic team. Why? Because the Clifton Strengths® assessment has the potential to uncover where the greatest personal potential lies. This methodology, coupled with debriefing with a professional Strengths coach, reveals *who* does *what* best.

Why is this important? Think of it this way, who wants to be on a team where its members feel dread and lack confidence? The individual and the collective team will ensure early and long-term wins when each person is contributing their best in the area they do best! Further, by cultivating these jagged edges, the team's capability is released.

A leadership coach who works with teams and certified in CliftonStrengths® moves this strategic process into action.

The assessment is derived from the perspective of Positive Psychology and developed by the late Don Clifton Ph.D., a pioneer researcher in the field of leadership. Dr. Clifton spent forty years studying great leaders.[182]Out of those leadership studies, the CliftonStrengths® assessment was born. Although there have been slight changes to the assessment since its initial unveiling in 2001, this assessment has changed the way organizations and individuals see themselves and collaborate. Since the assessment's inception, over 20 million people from countries around the globe have participated and uncovered their superpowers.

The assessment is composed of 177 pairs of potential self-descriptors and completed online. The standard Top 5 report generates a list of 5 dominant talent themes. To capture a greater appreciation of a leader's strength themes, purchasing the full 34 report is encouraged.

Once the assessment is complete, the strength themes are disseminated over four domains.[183]A Strengths coach helps leaders understand how their talent themes filter into four leadership domains and their significance. When leaders do not debrief their assessment with a Strengths coach, much is missed. Interpreting the report on your own is not suggested. Scheduling uninterrupted time to debrief your report in a 60-90 minute session will prove to be advantageous.

To gain a clearer understanding of how talents show up and are lived out in your professional and personal life, a Strength coach goes deeper than the words on the report. Additional sessions are encouraged to help support learning and implementation of the client's strengths so that the leader's strengths align with goal achievement. Strengths sessions create awareness so that the leader's contribution is maximized at work, home, and in the community they serve.

34 Strengths Themes and 4 Domains (Gallup®)

Executing	Influencing	Relationship Building	Strategic Thinking
Achiever	Activator	Adaptability	Analytical
Arranger	Command	Connectedness	Context
Belief	Communication	Developer	Futuristic
Consistency	Competition	Empathy	Ideation
Deliberative	Maximizer	Harmony	Input
Discipline	Self-Assurance	Includer	Intellection
Focus	Significance	Individualization	Learner
Responsibility	Woo	Positivity	Strategic
Restorative		Relator	

Sharpening Your Edge

CliftonStrengths® is a powerful tool to create awareness for each team member. When a team member understands their uniqueness, it creates a stronger version of the individual and, ultimately, the offering they bring to the talent table. However, this takes a Strengths coach who will lead the team member and group through a development process to uncover their mature strengths and talents that need further development.

> *Who wants to be on a team where team members feel dread and lack confidence?*

As with any assessment, debriefing with a professional coach is crucial. Assessments can offer insight for the client and the coach. However, the value of an assessment becomes diminished if a coach has little experience or is not certified in interpreting the results.[184] Debriefing with a Gallup® Certified Strengths Coach benefits the client. This debrief becomes the starting point toward using strengths strategies in the workplace.

When the organization strategically builds for strength, it is essential to look at who has what theme, but also ask what they do best. By asking this question, confidence is created for the individual, and the correct person is placed in the assignment that will best deliver the task best. This design sets the individual and the organization up for success.

A talent table provides a visual for the strategic team that is crafted by design. If possible, to build for success and diversity, all four strength domains should be accounted for with the team's Top 5. However, just because all domains are not accounted for, does not mean you will have an unsuccessful team. A Strengths coach will cast light on the domains for your team. There is more to domains than meets the eye.

The following table displays the team member and the *function* the team member will bring as their offering based on their dominant theme. The example that follows only identifies one talent theme per person. It is important to understand there are 33 other themes for each individual. This builds additional strength offerings into the talent table.

(Whelan, 2017; Adapted from Sorenson & Crabtree, 2001)[185]

Team Function	Contributor	Theme	What I Do Best
Leadership & Vision	Joon	Futuristic	Build the vision
Presents for team	Lina	Command	Take Charge
Goal Setting & Measurement	Amir	Maximizer	Prioritize-Make good; great
	Kai	Arranger	Set goals & Timelines
Communication	Ted & Rina	Communication & Arranger	Get the word out/ Update and circulate to-do list
Accountability	Matthias	Responsibility	Track meetings and follow-up
Selection/ Recognition	Dara	Individualization	Aligns fit with person

Through the initial coaching phase, the strategic team will gain an understanding of each individual's strengths and gain a greater appreciation for the diversity of the team as a whole. By encouraging a strengths approach to team-building, a more engaged, collaborative, trusting, peak performance talent team is created. When the coach and client work together to unpack and proactively work toward strengthening each person's dominant talents, the magic of building for strengths and sustainability occurs. Building with strengths is like casting a lamp to the team's feet to light their path. This path leads the team member to their unique seat at the talent table.

These individuals all have specific gifts. When those gifts are brought to the talent table, they become an offering.

According to the Merriam-Webster dictionary, the definition of an offering is:

"The act of one who offers." "Something offered; especially a sacrifice, ceremonially offered as part of worship."

The offering for a strategic team member is their *contribution*. Contribution per its definition is "a gift or payment to a common fund or collection" and "the part played by a person or thing in bringing about a result or helping something to advance." In a team effort, the contribution promotes the creation of a jagged edge team. A jagged edge team has an increased likelihood of effectively implementing strategy.

It is crucial to call on and bring your unique set of talents forth. In turn, you are to value the uniqueness of others. When a strategic team seeks to look through a strength's lens, the collective offering becomes a successful outcome.

Relational function and structure for strategy is imperative and often comes in the form of team-building. Team-building is as old as time. Whether we look to the NFL Draft or the best-selling book of all time, the Bible, both demonstrate strategic team-building.

NFL teams look to build for strength as they strategically choose talent to fill their roster. They research players and understand how players individual strengths help the collectiveness of the team.

The structure of this strategic initiative is similar to the historical relevance of Jesus choosing His twelve disciples. Like the leaders who build for strength by way of draft picks, Jesus sought after specific people to make up a 'team.' This team aligned with a mission and vision. Although I may be wrong, this author does not think Jesus randomly chose the twelve along the journey. He knew the gifts of each of His potential 'team members' and with intention, invited each one to follow. Just like the professional draft picks, the initial followers of Jesus were chosen by design.

When you're doing the choosing, do you do so by design or by default? An organization that establishes and manages performance by design creates a foundation for success. Designing for performance invites success at the onset and ensures alignment with the overall strategic objective. Building a high-performance team is not just made up of team members, but engaged contributors. When contributors unite, strength is built and excellence is the outcome.

Strengthening the Odds of Success

In an earlier chapter, pigeonholing was described. The practice of pigeonholing does not align with leadership excellence. Your people are never allowed the opportunity to rise and develop beyond their potential when they are contained by what you *think* they are capable of like the leader of Johnsonville Sausage implied.

Allowing your people to verbalize and demonstrate what they *are* capable of, or willing to try if given the tools to succeed requires an open, honest conversation.

Each of us is the expert of our self. Typically, you, the leader, know whether or not you are capable of carrying out an assignment, a project, or a role. Still, leaders often discount their capabilities and at times, cannot fully see what others see in them. Blind spots, decreased confidence levels, and self-sabotage contribute to misinterpreting your talents.

From a spiritual perspective, when we "deny our talents and instead focus on our weaknesses, on some level, we are telling God that we know best; He made a mistake in gracing us with our unique mix."[186]However, when employees become *contributors* by continuously developing their strengths, collaborative, goal-oriented relationships increase, and a talent team is born. This high-performance team is one that functions like a well-oiled machine because it is versed and immersed in strengths.

The role of the leader is to help others succeed. Developing your people is key to your leadership success. As a leader and team coach, I have the opportunity to support organizational development processes and implementation. These development processes create a competitive advantage by helping position high-performance strength teams for success. Although this team works with me, an external coach, an internal component of having a committed partnership is necessary.

When I have the opportunity to work with leaders, it's inspiring to witness teams look at themselves as a collective body incorporating a strengths approach to build for sustainability and success. When strengths work is encountered, conversations and actions start to change. When teams call on and call out each other's strengths, contributors experience an increased likelihood of attaining their collective goal, time after time.

> *Blind spots, decreased confidence levels, and self-sabotage contributes to misinterpreting your talents.*

The Coaching Corner

1. What is the current team-building strategy in your workplace? Are your teams built by design or by default?
2. What do *you* do best? How are you bringing what you do best to the talent table?
3. When was the last time you asked someone what *they* do best? What was their response?
4. What is one deliberate step you can take to position yourself as a contributor in the workplace?
5. How can team-building by design benefit your next strategic effort?
6. When was a time you were part of a high performing team?
7. What made the team perform at a high level?
8. How can a professional coach help guide your strategic initiative?

Chapter 11

Leading Virtual Teams

"The speed of the boss is the speed of the team."
~Lee Iacocca

In today's tech-savvy world, the workplace is no longer utilizing only in-person options for communicating across channels. With advancements in technology, anyone with an internet connection has the ability to participate from any corner of the world.

Between the years of 2011-2017, I spent much of my advanced education in the virtual space. Although I thrived, it was not without a communication learning curve.

For me, it took dedication to learn the ins and outs of the platform used for communicating. It also took being open to a new way of "showing up" to learn. The virtual space allowed me to expand my learning and interact with leaders across the globe.

Although geographically dispersed with time zone and cultural differences, engaging in virtual communication has become the norm, being more widely used and accepted. The six years I spent in the virtual classroom prepared me to serve my clients, who are many times geographically dispersed.

A Society for Human Research Management (SHRM) survey stated that nearly half of the polled organizations claim to have used virtual teams. Multi-national companies were identified as more likely to use remote teams than US-based companies (68% vs. 28%). Additional research identifies 70% of today's workers are remote at least one day a week. According to FlexJobs and Global Workplace Analytics, 3.4% of the population (4.7 million) work in the virtual space.

Creating A Competitive Advantage

A competitive advantage in business is a concept that cannot be sedentary. An organization must continually be reinventing itself, setting itself apart from its competitors, and acquire a sustainable, competitive edge. Studies show there are many potential advantages to working in virtual teams such as increased creativity, finding acceptance of new ideas through an interconnected group, and developing culturally synergistic results. Other benefits include lower travel expenses, labor costs, and assembling teams quickly from any location.

By-products of virtual teams include reducing the companies' carbon footprint and accommodating flexible work schedules. However, with great capability, great challenges arise. As individuals and teams strive to communicate effectively in a global world, they are often at the mercy of technology, which at times creates ineffective communication.

In addition, email and text messaging are primary communication methods for many organizations. Because of this, there is an open door for miscommunication that often lead to failed outcomes.

For the first time in history, multiple generations are working together. This means there are different communication styles. Although we acknowledge generational differences, most people do not adapt their communication approach to align with who they are communicating. This lack of adaptation creates additional barriers to how communication is received and perceived. Just as the need to develop cross-cultural relationships have importance, leaders must develop and understand communication amongst the generations.

Risks For Teams

Although there are many benefits for assembling virtual teams, there are potential risks that impact performance as well as team experience. Potential risks create weakness. Lack of face to face meetings (which are especially crucial in the beginning stages), cultural diversity, language barriers, insufficient technical skills, lack of project management skills/leadership, and time zone differences can all lead to a failed team experience.

The human factor creates a multitude of challenges, to include: building trust, establishing relationships, developing competent intercultural communication, team leadership, managing global team dynamics, and accountability. Intra-team conflict is often triggered by a lack of healthy communication, which leaves team performance impacted.

Virtual team members often have uncertainties about their team members due to a lack of visual cues. However, these uncertainties become diminished when interpersonal trust is established.

Visual Cue Impact

In contrast to face to face teams who have communication with team members and are privy to visual cues, the lack of social cues for virtual teams can have a negative impact. Team members find a lack of visual cues, both visual and verbal, amplify circumstances, and open the team up for conflict.

Geographically dispersed virtual teams tend to have less organizational affiliation due to the absence of cues. When the ability to impact emotions, voice tone, and self-expression is constrained, the lack of these nonverbal and para verbal cues [how we *say* the words] may lead to a breakdown in team communication in the virtual environment.

From this author's personal experience, when there is a lack of communication and preparation, the spirit of a virtual team becomes muddled and disorganized. The challenges that virtual teams face can create discontent and decrease performance unless high impact strategies are implemented.

When all parts continually function together, there is less of a likelihood for a failed attempt to operationalize a team. All the pieces must work synergistically, and to be successful, a company must evolve in the way they communicate to the workplace.

Assessing how the team communicates is not a once and done activity. Just as a strategic plan must be reassessed with time, so does creating capabilities that will continuously be supported and changed as needed. In the world of virtual communication, capabilities must be established to produce results-driven teams.

Preparing & Strategizing For Success

The preparation phase is a unique way to create an advantage in the area of virtual global team effectiveness. Key aspects of this phase include developing a team mission statement, task design, rewards system, appropriate technology [including training], and organization integration.

An effective initial design and launch phase helps with the success of the team. An integral part of a successful virtual team includes a kickoff workshop to get acquainted, convey goals, clarify expectations, and development intra-team rules. This phase may take longer than face to face teams.

Research suggests creating a virtual team charter. The charter includes the team's mission, core values, business problem, and objectives of the team.

The charter also includes:
- clear individual and team goals
- rules of engagement, ground rules, boundaries
- information sharing practices
- meeting attendance, and,
- an explicit group agreement of the team's long-term goals

Virtual team members have better performance outcomes when shared knowledge is blended amongst group members. Cohesion and unity are birthed out of a collective purpose.

Activities that include virtual peer communication must be strategically laid out for all team members to have a clear, concise understanding of their objectives. Incorporating a Standard Operating Procedure (SOP) will reduce time and unnecessary intervention once the team proceeds.

A shared understanding allows for team collaboration and consistency. Without this measure, there is less ability to predict group and individual behaviors. The SOP is similar to the measure an organization takes with its organizational safeguards, as discussed in Chapter 5.

Task design is a structural tool and impacts remote teams. Remote teams do not have the advantage of seeing a team member in the hallway to discuss a detail or unclear expectation. Rules that clearly state the basis for communicating must be overseen and managed with a constant effort. Trivial details down to e-mail response rules must be established. Individual and team performance is inhibited by a lack of goal adherence, which leaves opportunity for undisciplined behavior. It is up to team leaders to continually keep the team on task.

Heading Off Conflict

Constructing strategies on how conflict is addressed and tasks are distributed creates a collaborative decision-making process. This decreases task confusion and increases the project's success rate. Task conflict is often an indicator reflecting a positive correlation between task conflict and perceived team performance in teams with high virtuosity.

Additionally, how tasks are performed leads to process conflict and negatively impacts the perceived team performance. The progress towards a team goal is diminished when disagreements of how to proceed amongst virtual team members conflicts. Having clear, concise goals are essential for face to face teams and become even more critical for teams who work virtually. Tasks that are specific or have special goals may experience less task conflict. Task-related conflict is minimized through transparent task instructions and a clear distribution of responsibility.

The Human Factor

It's important to remember the human factor when thinking of implementing a virtual environment for your team members, or you're already utilizing this capability. Teams are made up of people with feelings, emotions, and egos. These cannot and should not be discounted. It's up to the leader to be the example of how the team proceeds or continues to operate. A positive leadership example, as well as a clear path for the team will increase the likelihood of success.

Organizational Identification

Organizational identification refers to the degree to which the company and the team share the same values, goals, desires, and aims.

The amount of organizational identification a person has with their team reduces uncertainty. Identification is especially relevant for cross-cultural, remote teams where the level of virtuosity often indicates the level of identification that one has with the organization and the team itself.

Higher levels of identification are found to have positive effects on the team with increased motivation, higher cooperation, job satisfaction, lower group conflict, and more group cohesion. These higher levels are found with team members who have a collectivist background. Collectivist cultures are often referred to as having a kinship. Lower levels of organizational identification tend to have an individualistic cultural background where working alone is the norm.

Affiliation and organizational identification, whether a team member is collectivist or individualist, contribute to team performance.

Accountability Through Peer Reviews

A peer review is a useful tool to identify individual and virtual group activity performance. Peer assessments have been shown to increase attitudes and accomplishments. The window the team assesses captures internal work processes that may not be readily apparent to the team leader.

When peer feedback is used to evaluate the actions and performance of group members, motivation, interaction, cooperation, and satisfaction increases.[187]

Timeliness matters. When teams neglect to develop and implement strategic touchpoints during their preparation phase, feedback is lost. Team evaluations should be completed incrementally to keep abreast of any potential problems and necessary interventions. Those who practice providing feedback to group members, as well as participate in assessing their own performance, are better prepared for evaluations in the workplace. The foundational skill of assessing leader and team member contribution generates responsibility and accountability.

A peer review is a development activity that aids the overall team process. Peer evaluations tend to increase reliability and reduce biases that become evident in singular evaluations. The team member experience is a "privileged viewpoint" and lends itself to being a well-informed source of insight. This form of self and other evaluation helps uncover strengths and blind spots of the remote team.

Peer evaluations in the workplace should be well-accepted practices that promote learning and growth. In general, peer reviews are confidential.

The following categories are a starting point when considering the development of an evaluation: work quality, team contributions, cooperation, conceptual contribution, and work ethic.[188] Incorporating a strengths lens to the assessment allows a strengths team to recognize and celebrate their team's use of strengths.

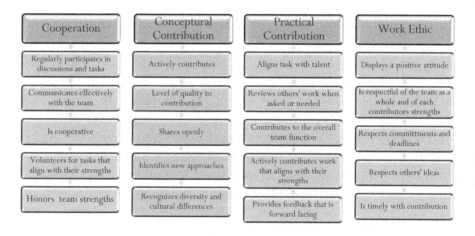

Research conducted by Donia and Burns suggests raters should justify peer evaluations if the scoring for an individual is less than a 4 on the 5-point scale.[189] Justification aids in accountability. The outcome provides a fuller picture for the recipient and team lead when reviews go beyond a number.

Establishing a centralized peer assessment is significant in team effectiveness. There is heightened motivation when team members expect an evaluation. When team members read their reviews in transcript form, it provides an individual learning experience and prepares teams for 360 feedback assessments that are widely used in the 21st-century workplace.

Social Loafing

Tasks that are designed to lend themselves to a shared knowledge structure and interdependence of all virtual team members reduce social loafing. Social loafing is a consistent unacceptable behavior that virtual teams contend with that is counterproductive. Social loafing, also known as coasting, is when a team member or members continually fail to follow procedures or meet deadlines. This common complaint is hedged by providing peer evaluations to help deter this process and increase accountability.

Enacting a peer review as a requirement for team members assists with providing a positive team experience and curtails social loafing.

Critical Components For Teams

Researchers describe several competencies for virtual teams to consider. Collectively, researchers identify important influences and characteristics which enhanced the virtual team experience.

For any team to be effective, time and effort must be given to its design, as demonstrated by the components outlined in the figure that follows. For teams to provide excellence from inception, each area must be acknowledged and planned.

With advances in technology, virtual teams have the opportunity to be face to face while still working remotely. This 21st-century way of communicating adds a crucial element and once missing piece for effective functioning teams. Investing in a communication platform that allow face to face visual cues is imperative. This author believes no team should be without the opportunity to participate in face to face meetings and experience the richness it provides. What do *you* think?

The Coaching Corner

1. What is your experience with virtual teams or the virtual environment?
2. What made the experience successful or not successful?
3. What is your experience with social loafing? How has social loafing affected a project or team outcome?
4. What accountability measures are built into your virtual team experience?
5. How do you measure success for your virtual team?
6. When you look at the figure that outlines effective team components, what does your team do well, and what needs improvement?

Chapter 12

Living Your Leadership Legacy

"Carve your name on hearts, not tombstones."
~Shannon Alder

It is by no accident that you are called to leadership. Our fast-moving, corrupt world needs authentic, courageous leaders like you —leaders who are willing to accept the calling and incorporate principles of excellence.

However, creating excellence by design must go beyond contemplating the words and illustrations within the chapters of this book. It is not enough. Building excellence within the walls of your organization, community, and your home takes action.

Leaders who practice excellence want to be successful. They desire to create meaning and purpose for their life, but also for others. In our performance-driven world where individuals are retained or rejected sometimes on the spot, the positive impact they have in the workplace many times ends prematurely.

This author believes even in adversity; all circumstances work for good. As leaders, we are asked to impact the world right where we are planted, regardless of the natural circumstance we see or experience. Therefore, as a leader, you are in control and responsible for your leadership legacy, including the living narrative you portray to the world.

Pledging Your Legacy

Living your legacy takes *pledging* your legacy. Leaders are familiar with aligning company mission, values, and casting visions for their organization. These bring clarity to internal and external partners and are crucial steps for strategic excellence. But, have you ever considered writing a *personal* vision, mission, or values statement and pledge? Creating a solid leadership legacy statement and pledge encompasses your personal mission, vision, and values.

The earlier a leader considers her or his legacy and pledges alignment, the better chance of becoming a better leader!

Legacy statement and pledge planning is not succession planning or replacement planning. Instead, it provides an opportunity to meditate on your values, goals, and beliefs.

A legacy pledge statement can be one sentence, a paragraph, or several pages.

A legacy statement is:
- unique to self
- brings clarity to who you are as a leader, and/or who you pledge to become
- inspires leaders to reach a higher level of commitment to the call of leadership

Your legacy statement is written from your heart and is a process that should not be rushed. The ethical safeguards for your organization discussed in Chapter 5 are intended to be *practiced,* not placed in a drawer or hidden in a closet. The same is true for your leadership legacy pledge. Your legacy statement is a living, breathing document that provides direction, and at times, *self-correction* to re-align yourself with who you say you are.

Rest and self-care are also principles of excellence. Now is the time to put these principles into practice as you carve out uninterrupted time to process through your current and future self.

The only wrong way to approach this exercise is not to complete it. As you proceed, consider the following:
- What do I want to project to the world?
- What is important to me?

For faith leaders:
- How do faith practices intersect and enrich my leadership?
- What scripture aligns with my current or projected leadership?

As you read the example below, ask yourself:
Do the words give you an understanding of who this leader strives to be?

Legacy Pledge Example

I seek to clearly communicate my leadership by being a living example of a humble, moral, leader of excellence.

To be an innovative visionary and courageous trailblazer.

To pour into, empower, and encourage others so they, in turn, can do the same.

To establish and support an environment where mutual trust and respect is practiced; and where others thrive.

Regardless of rank, nationality, age, or religion, I will value and embrace the differences in others.

I will craft cultures where individual and organizational potential is realized, maximized, and surpassed, and where leaders are developed and strengthened by uncovering and positioning their gifts and talents for the greater good.

I will build bridges when faced with adversity and continually lead from a posture of authenticity; leaning into transformational principles of leadership excellence.

The Authentic Leader

When you deliberately lead from the point of legacy, it positions you toward authenticity. This authenticity guides your daily actions. The authentic leader influences and creates impact for those around them because they understand their purpose. They lead with both head and heart, are self-disciplined, establish fruitful relationships, and have solidified their values. Their authenticity becomes their natural repeated response in and outside the workplace. Their character demonstrates integrity.

A Time to Rise

If you truly want to impact tomorrow, *you must start today*. The time is now to challenge yourself and those around you to rise and walk out your leadership right where you are. You are called to make a difference in this world, to leave the world a better place, and to demonstrate the principles of leadership excellence. Our world is begging for strong, courageous, confident leaders. By authentically leading yourself and your people, you *can* change the world!

Are you ready?

The Coaching Corner

1. When you leave the room, the meeting, current position, or this earth, how do you want to be remembered?
2. Is how you want to be remembered in each of the above instances the same or different? Why or why not?
3. What descriptive words come to mind when you think about what your leadership reflects to others? What needs crafting?
4. How can a legacy statement support your leadership direction and narrative?
5. Who besides you will benefit from your legacy statement?
6. How can a professional coach help you design and develop your individual and organizational level of excellence?
7. What is one leadership practice you will start doing, and one you will stop doing after reading this book?
8. What is the biggest take-away from this book and why?
9. Which chapter helped your leadership the most? How so?

Acknowledgements

Writing and publishing *Leadership Excellence By Design* did not happen without the support of many people who believed in the message found within. I would like to acknowledge those who walked with me, either directly or indirectly. It is because of each of you that I am blessed.

To the One who tells me I can do all things, my Creator. Thank you for the guidance of the Holy Spirit who gave me supernatural endurance and direction when I needed it most.

Thank you, M.G. "Pat" Robertson, Founder, Chancellor, and CEO of Regent University, for providing the space to advance my leadership studies.

To the professors and mentors who prayed me through life events that would have otherwise derailed me from finishing the good work He had started in me. Your unwavering support was instrumental in completing my doctoral work, this book, and my what's next.

To the leaders who gave their time and shared their wisdom, thank you for being a *leader of leaders*.

To the community of leaders who journey with me; you were created to lead with confidence. Keep doing great things and *let's build confident leaders together*!

GETMO!

About the Author

Dr. Kelly Whelan is the Founder of Belem Leaders and is an internationally recognized executive and team coach, and leadership advisor. Dr. Whelan specializes in individual and organizational assessment, design, and development services. She brings guidance and insight to help her clients identify and maximize personal, professional, and corporate goals.

Kelly's passion for leadership excellence and professional growth led her into executive coaching and leadership development. Her ability to work cooperatively across diverse environments with all levels of leadership has made her a sought-after leadership development advisor.

Dr. Whelan gives back to her community by serving in volunteer leadership roles at her local church, sits on various committees, and hosts the Global Leadership Summit simulcast in Naples, Florida.

Kelly holds a Doctorate in Strategic Leadership with a concentration in Leadership Coaching from Regent University, a Master of Administration with a concentration in Leadership from Central Michigan University, and is certified through the Gallup® organization as a Strengths Coach.

Dr. Whelan is a devoted wife, mother of 3, and cherishes every moment she shares with her precious grandsons.

BelemLeaders

Let's build confident leaders together.

Leadership & CliftonStrengths® Seminars & Workshops

Executive Coaching

Team and Group Coaching

Organization-wide and Individual Leader Assessments

Consulting Services

Keynotes

Author-led Book Study

Dr. Kelly M.G. Whelan

Coming soon! Coaching Excellence By Design

References

1 Northouse, P. (2013). Leadership theory and practice. Thousand Oaks, CA: Sage.

2 Winston, B., & Patterson, K. (2006). An integrative definition of leadership. International Journal of Leadership Studies , 1(2), 6-66.

3 Kuhn, T. (2012). The structure of scientific revolutions. Chicago, IL: The University of Chicago Press.

4 Gallup® (2018). Exit Programs That Retain Stars and Brand Ambassadors.

5 Oster, G. (2011).

6 Kuyper, A. (2011). Wisdom & wonder: Common grace in science & art. Grand Rapids, MI: Christian's Library Press.

7 Berkun, S. (2010). The myths of innovation. Sebastopol, CA.: O'Reilly Media.

8 Houghton, J. D., & DiLiello, T. C. (2010). Leadership development: The key to unlocking individual creativity in organizations. Leadership & Organization Development Journal, 31(3), 230-245.

9 Perrin, C., Perrin, P. B., Blauth, C., Apthorp, E., Duffy, R. D., Bonterre, M., & Daniels, S. (2012). Factor analysis of global trends in 21st century leadership. Leadership & Organization Development Journal, 33(2), 175-199.

10 Oster, G. (2015). Creativity and Innovation. [Dialogue 4A]. Retrieved from https://regent.blackboard.com/webapps/blackboard/content/listContent.jsp?course_id=_130236_1&content_id=_4926505_1

11 Davila, T., Epstein, M., & Shelton, R. (2006).

12 ibid.

13 Stefano, S. F., & Wasylyshyn, K. M. (2005). Integrity, courage, empathy (ICE): Three leadership essentials. HR.Human Resource Planning, 28(4), 5-7.

14 Filipczak, B. (1997). It takes all: Creativity in the work force. Training. 34(5), 32-40

15 Brunner, G. F. (2001). The Tao of innovation. Research Technology Management, 44(1), 45-51.

16 Loewe, P., & Dominiquini, J. (2006).

17 Davila, T., Epstein, M., & Shelton, R. (2006).

18 Ibid.

19 Leavy, B. (2005). A leader's guide to creating an innovation culture. Strategy & Leadership, 33(4), 38-45.

20 Huffington Post (March 28, 2008 & May 25th 2011) Spitzer prostitution scandal: NY Gov admits links to sex. [Webpage] Retrieved from https://www.huffingtonpost.com/2008/03/10/spitzer-prostitution-scan_n_90766.htmlring.

21 Fox News (November 6, 2017). Anthony Weiner to begin prison sentence for sexting conviction. Retrieved from http://www.foxnews.com/politics/2017/11/06/anthony-weiner-to-begin-prison-sentence-for-sexting-conviction.html

22 The Washington Post (January 12, 2017). Three Takata executives charged in global airbag scandal. Retrieved from https://www.engadget.com/2017/01/13/three-takata-executives-charged-in-global-airbag-scandal/

23 Office of Oversight and Investigations Minority Staff Report (Feb 23, 2016) Total Recall: Internal documents detail Takata's broken safety culture and the need for a more effective recall process. Retrieved from [Addendum]https://www.commerce.senate.gov/public/_cache/files/04c489c1-36e8-4037-b60b-c50285f3e436/5D6F21C6E25F0702634A24422FA92CEC.2-23-16-final-takata-addendum-and-exhibits.pdf

24 The Washington Post (September 22, 2015). VW emissions cheating affects 11 million cars worldwide. [Webpage] Retrieved from https://www.washingtonpost.com/business/economy/vw-emissions-cheating-affects-11-million-cars-worldwide/2015/09/22/30f59bca-6126-11e5-9757-e49273f05f65_story.html?tid=a_inl&utm_term=.83e6e64f7905

25 The New York Times (August 4, 2017). Volkswagen executive pleads guilty in diesel emissions case. [Web News] Retrieved from https://www.nytimes.com/2017/08/04/business/volkswagen-diesel-oliver-schmidt.html

26 CNN Money (July 1, 2015). Toyota executive Julie Hamp resigns after narcotics arrest. Retrieved from http://money.cnn.com/2015/07/01/autos/toyota-executive-oxycodone-resigns/index.html

27 USA Today (July 8, 2015). Toyota exec released, won't be charged in drug case. [Web News] Retrieved from https://www.usatoday.com/story/money/cars/2015/07/08/julie-hamp-released-toyota/29852095/

28 Hofstede, G., Hofstede, J., and Minkov, M. (2010). Cultures and organizations: Software of the mind. USA: McGraw Hill.

29 Arjoon, S. (2010). Narcissistic behavior and the economy: The role of virtues. Journal of Markets and Morality, 13(1).

30 Rosenbaum, S. M., Billinger, S., & Stieglitz, N. (2013). Private virtues, public vices: Social norms and corruption. *International Journal of Development Issues*, 12(3), 192-212.

31 Rawwas, M. Y. A., & Isakson, H. R. (2000). Ethics of tomorrow's business managers: The influence of personal beliefs and values, individual characteristics, and situational factors. *Journal of Education for Business*, 75(6), 321-330.

32 Thompson, L. J. (2010). The global moral compass for business leaders. *Journal of Business Ethics*, 93, 15-32.

33 Baltact, A. (2017). Reasons for whistleblowing. *Journal of Educational Sciences Research*. No. 1.

34 CNN *VA whistle-blower tells all about secret wait list* (June 23, 2014) [YouTube]Retrieved from https://www.youtube.com/watch?v=g2tW7HHvKS4

35 USA Today (April 7, 2016) *VA bosses in 7 states falsified vets' wait times for care.*[Website] Retrieved from https://www.usatoday.com/story/news/politics/2016/04/07/va-wait-time-manipulation-veterans/82726634/

36 Losey, M., Meisinger, S., & Ulrich, D. (2005). *The future of human resource management.* Hoboken, NJ: John Wiley & Sons.

37 Wright, N. T. (2012). *After you Believe: Why Christian Character Matters.* [video] Retrieved from: https://www.youtube.com/watch?v=ukyNU51OcnA

38 Hackett, R. D., & Wang, G. (2012). Virtues and leadership. *Management Decision*, 50(5), 868-899

39 Fedler, K. (2006). *Exploring Christian ethics: Biblical foundations for morality.* Louisville, KY: Westminster John Knox Press.

40 Hackett, R. D., & Wang, G. (2012).

41 Hackman, M. & Johnson, C. (2009). *Leadership communication perspective.* (5th Ed) Waveland Press.

42 Fedler, K. (2006).

43 Johnson, C. (2012).

44 Fedler, K. (2006). p. 44.

45 Ibid.

46 Ciulla, J.B. (2004). *Ethics: The heart of leadership.* Westport, CT: Praeger Publishers.

47 Losey, M., Meisinger, S., & Ulrich, D. (2005).

48 Caldwell, C., & Karri, R. (2005). Organizational governance and ethical systems: A covenantal approach to building trust. *Journal of Business Ethics*, 58(1-3), 249-259.

50 Hultman, K. (2002).

51 Caldwell, C., Dixon, R., Atkins, R., & Dowdell, S. (2011). Repentance and continuous improvement: Ethical implications for the modern leader. *Journal of Business Ethics*, 102(3), 473-487.

52 Nouwen, H. M. (2002). In the name of Jesus : Reflections on Christian leadership. New York: Crossroad Publishing Co.

53 The New York Times (May 19, 2017). *Weiner pleads guilty to federal obscenity charges.* [Web News]. Retrieved from https://www.nytimes.com/2017/05/19/nyregion/anthony-weiner-guilty-plea-sexting.html

54 Politico (May 24, 2016). *VA secretary I 'deeply regret' if I offended vets* [Web News] Retrieved from https://www.politico.com/story/2016/05/robert-mcdonald-no-disneyland-apology-223523

55 The Daily News, May 7, 2019: Ex-Purdue Pharma CEO Richard Sackler called opioid addicts 'scum,' 'criminals' in emails Retrieved from: https://www.nydailynews.com/news/national/ny-news-richard-sackler-opioid-addicts-scum-criminals-emails-20190507-ujfmvpphqjc77icemxafbjhlai-story.html

56 Caldwell, C., Dixon, R., Atkins, R., & Dowdell, S. (2011)..

57 Northouse, P. (2013).

58 Caldwell, C., Dixon, R., Atkins, R., & Dowdell, S. (2011).

59 Deloitte (2018). *Human Global Capital Trends 2018* [Report].Retrieved from: https://www2.deloitte.com/insights/us/en/focus/human-capital-trends.html

60 Deloitte (2017). *Human Global Capital Trends 2017* [Report] Retrieved from https://www2.deloitte.com/us/en/pages/human-capital/articles/introduction-human-capital-trends.html

61 Pew Research Center (2019). Defining generations: Where Millennials end and Generation Z begins. Retrieved from: https://www.pewresearch.org/fact-tank/2019/01/17/where-millennials-end-and-generation-z-begins/

62 Deloitte (2017).

63 Nuntamanop, P., Kauranen, I., & Igel, B. (2013). A new model of strategic thinking competency. *Journal of Strategy and Management*, 6(3), 242-264.

64 Losey et al., (2005). p. 367.

65 Pew Research Center (2016) *The State of American Jobs: How the shifting economic landscape is reshaping work and society and affecting the way people think about the skills and training they need to get ahead.* [Report]. Retrieved from http://assets.pewresearch.org/wp-content/uploads/sites/3/2016/10/ST_2016.10.06_Future-of-Work_FINAL4.pdf

66 Schein, (2010).

67 DeSilva, D. A. (2004).

68 R. J. Thomas, J. Bellin, C. Jules, & N. Lynton (2013). Developing tomorrow's global leaders. *MIT Sloan Management Review*, (2013): 55(1), 12-13.

69 Hunt, J.M. & Weintraub, J.R., (2007). The coaching organization: A strategy for developing leaders. Thousand Oaks: CA: Sage Publications, Inc.

70 McCauley, C., Kanaga, K., & Lafferty, K. (2010). Leader Development Systems. In The Center for Creative Leadership handbook of leadership development (3rd ed., pp. 29-61). San Francisco, CA: Jossey-Bass.

71 Myatt, M. (2012, December). The #1 reason leadership development fails. Forbes. Retrieved from http://www.forbes.com/sites/mikemyatt/2012/12/19/the-1-reason-leadership-development-fails/#7606986034ce

72 Hartsfield, M. (2015, September 17). 15FA LDSL 733 *leadership development collaborate session* 2. Retrieved from https://regent.blackboard.com/webapps/bb-collaboratebb_bb60/recording/play?course_id=_130106_1&recordingId=8754247&recordingFormat=1

73 Frankovelgia, C., & Riddle, D. (2010). *Leadership coaching.* In The center for creative leadership: Handbook of leadership development (3rd ed., pp. 125-146). San Francisco, CA: Jossey-Bass.

74 Crabb, S. (2011). The use of coaching principles to foster employee engagement. *The Coaching Psychologist*, 7(1), 27-34.

75 Kaye, B. & Crowell, B. (2012). *Coaching for engagement and retention* In Coaching for Leadership. (3rd ed., pp. 165-171). San Francisco, CA: Pfeiffer.

77 Gallup® (2017) *State of the American Workplace* [Report]. http://www.gallup.com/reports/199961/state-american-workplace-report-2017.aspx

78 http://www.gallup.com/services/190118/engaged-workplace.aspx

79 Gallup® (2017).

80 Gallup® *The relationship between engagement at work and organizational outcomes: 2016 Q12 Meta-analysis*: Nine Edition. ; Gallup® (2017) *State of the American Workplace* [Report]. http://www.gallup.com/reports/199961/state-american-workplace-report-2017.aspx

81 McCauley, C., Kanaga, K., & Lafferty, K. (2010).

83 Gallup® (2017), p. 63.

84 Kaye, B. & Crowell, B. (2012)..

85 Harter (2017, April 27) [*The Gallup Blog*] Retrieved from http://www.gallup.com/opinion/gallup/208691/failed-performance-management-fix.aspx?utm_source=alert&utm_medium=email&utm_content=morelink&utm_campaign=syndication

86 Gallup® (2017)

87 Hooijberg, R. & Lane, N. (Summer 2016) How Boards botch CEO succession. *MIT Sloan Review*, 57(4), 14-16.

88 Ibid.

89 Rothwell, W. (2010). *Effective succession planning: Ensuring leadership continuity and building talent from within.* New York, NY: Amacom.

91 Ip, B., & Jacobs, G. (2006). Business succession planning: A review of the evidence. *Journal of Small Business and Enterprise Development*, 13(3), 326-350.

92 Rice, G. (2007). Elijah's requirement for prophetic leadership (2 Kings 2:1-18). *Journal Of Religious Thought*, 59-60(1-1), 1-12.

93 Ibid.

94 Schein, E. (2010). *Organizational culture and leadership*. San Francisco, CA: Jossey-Bass. p. 281.

95 Rothwell, W. (2010).

96 https://www.spencerstuart.com/~/media/sp500ceotransitions_q1q2%202017_updated%208%209%2017.pdf

97 Hooijberg, R. & Lane, N. (Summer 2016) .

98 Conger, J. A., & Nadler, D. A. (2004). When CEOs step up to fail. *MIT Sloan Management Review*, 45(3), 50-56.

99 Korn Ferry Institute (n.d.) *The risky business of CEO succession.* Retrieved from https://www.kornferry.com/institute/download/view/id/8329/aid/996

100 https://www.nationwide.com/about-us/020717-nw-business-succession.jsp

101 Al-Asfour, A., & Lettau, L. (2014). Strategies for leadership styles for multi-generational workforce. *Journal of Leadership, Accountability and Ethics*, 11(2), 58-69.

102 Gibson, J. W., Greenwood, R. A., & Murphy, Edward F. Jr. (2009). Generational differences in the workplace: Personal values, behaviors, and popular beliefs. *Journal of Diversity Management*, 4(3), 1-7.

103 Ibid.

104 Ferri-Reed, J. (2013). Quality, conflict, and communication across the generations. *The Journal for Quality and Participation*, 35(4), 12-14.

105 Gibson, J. W., Greenwood, R. A., & Murphy, Edward F. Jr. (2009).

106 Ibid.

107 Ferri-Reed, J. (2013)..

108 Gallup (2017).

109 Ibid.

110 U.S. Securities and Exchange Commission [Proposed Rule] retrieved from https://www.sec.gov/rules/proposed/2016/ia-4439.pdf

111 U.S. Securities And Exchange Commission [Comments on Proposed Rule] Retrieved from https://www.sec.gov/comments/s7-13-16/s71316.htm

112 Cornish, E. (2004). *Futuring: The exploration of the future*. Bethesda, MD: World Future.

113 The New York Times (June 21, 2015) *How Survey Monkey is Coping After the Death of Dave Goldberg*. Retrieved from https://www.nytimes.com/2015/06/22/technology/how-surveymonkey-is-coping-after-death-of-dave-goldberg.html

114 Hooijberg, R. & Lane, N. (Summer 2016).

115 Ibid.

116 *Laurie Departs GoPro to Take CEO job at Survey Monkey* (January 13, 2016) Retrieved from https://www.recode.net/2016/1/13/11588778/lurie-departs-gopro-to-take-ceo-job-at-surveymonkey

117 Ibid.

118 Hooijberg, R. & Lane, N. (Summer 2016).

119 http://www.stltoday.com/business/jai-nagarkatti-sigma-aldrich-ceo-dies-at/article_46d399bc-61e2-521a-9ff8-b7048bf6ab3b.html

120 Hooijberg, R. & Lane, N. (Summer 2016).

121 Losey, M., Meisinger, S., & Ulrich, D. (2005).

122 Ibid.

123 Ackermann, F. & Eden, C. *Making Strategy: Mapping Out Strategic Success* (Thousand Oaks: Sage Publications Ltd.)

124 Sarah L. Simoneaux and Chris L. Stroud. "Business Best Practices: SWOT Analysis: The Annual Check-Up for a Business." *Journal of Pension Benefits* 18, no. 3 (Spring, 2011): 75-78.

125 Hughes, R., & Beatty, K. (2005). *Becoming a strategic leader*. San Francisco, CA: Jossey Bass.

126 Ackermann & Eden (2011).

127 Ibid.

128 Hughes, R., & Beatty, K. (2005).

129 Ibid.

130 Ackermann & Eden (2011).

131 Moore, J. R., Kizer, L. E., & Jeon, B. P. (2011). Leading groups to create healthy culture through accomplishing tasks aligned to strategy. *International Journal of Management and Information Systems*, 15(2), 55-64.

132. Ackermann & Eden (2011).

133 Hughes, R., & Beatty, K. (2005).

134 Thompson, John and Melissa Cole. 1997. "Strategic Competency - the Learning Challenge." *Journal of Workplace Learning* 9 (5): 153-162.

135 Hu, Qing, Pauline Found, Sharon Williams, and Robert Mason. 2014. "The Role of Consultants in Organizational Learning." *Journal of Management Policy and Practice* 15 (4): 29-39.

136 Hughes, R., & Beatty, K. (2005).

137 Ibid.

138 Winston, B., & Patterson, K. (2006).

139 Nuntamanop, P., Kauranen, I., & Igel, B. (2013).

140 Hughes, R., & Beatty, K. (2005).

141 Ibid.

142 Grant, A. (2012).

143 Dewar, J. A. (2002). *Assumption-based planning*. New York: Cambridge University Press. pp. 1-13.

146 Stayer, R. (2009).

147 Canton, J. (2007). *Extreme future*. New York, NY: Penguin Group.

148 Cornish, E. (2004).

149 Gobble, M. M. (2012). Innovation and strategy. *Research Technology Management*, 55(3), 63-67.

150 Vaiman, V., Scullion, H., & Collings, D. (2012). Talent management decision making. *Management Decision*, 50(5), 925-941.

151 Slaughter, R. A. (1993). *Futures concepts. Futures*, 25(3), 289-315.

152 Millett, S. M. (2006). Futuring and visioning: Complementary approaches to strategic decision making. *Strategy & Leadership*, 34(3), 43-50.

153 Hughes, R., & Beatty, K. (2005).

154 Ibid.

155 Ackermann, F., & Eden, C. (2011).

156 Tibbs, H. (1999). *Making the future visible: Psychology, scenarios, and strategy*. Canberra, Australia: Australian Public Service Futures Group. Retrieved from: http://www.hardintibbs.com/wp-content/uploads/2009/10/future-landscape-tibbs-a4.pdf

157 Hu, Qing, P. F., Williams, S. & Mason, R. (2014). The Role of Consultants in Organizational Learning. *Journal of Management Policy and Practice* 15 (4): 29-39.

158 Lingenfelter, (2008). Management and organizational development. *The Journal of Management Development,* 32(1), 65.

159 Cabrera, A., & Unruh, G. (2012).

160 Hughes, R., & Beatty, K. (2005).

161 Mukherjee, D., Hanlon, S., Kedia, B., & Srivastava, P. (2012). Organizational identification among global virtual team members. *Cross Cultural Management*, 526-545.

162 Oster, G. (2011). *The light prize: Perspectives on Christian innovation*. Virginia Beach, VA: Positive Signs Media.

163 Loewe, P., & Dominiquini, J. (2006). Overcoming the barriers to effective innovation. *Strategy & Leadership*, 34(1), 24-31.

164 Davila, T., Epstein, M., & Shelton, R. (2006). *Making innovation work*. Upper Saddle River, NJ: Wharton School Publishing.

165 Oster, G. (2011)..

166 Hughes, R., & Beatty, K. (2005).

167 Abdulkarim, R. M. (2013). *The relationship between a leader's self-perceived level of emotional intelligence and organizational climate, as perceived by organizational members*. (Order No. 3587854).

168 Burton, R., Obel, B., & DeSanctis, C., (2011). *Organizational design: A step by step approach*. Cambridge University Press: NY

169 Ibid.

170 Rusly, F. H., Corner, J. L., & Sun, P. (2012). Positioning change readiness in knowledge management research. *Journal of Knowledge Management*, 16(2), 329-355.

171 Hughes, R., & Beatty, K. (2005).

172 Rusly, F. H., Corner, J. L., & Sun, P. (2012).

173 Chermack, T. J. (2011). *Scenario planning in organizations*. San Francisco, CA: Berrett-Koehler Publishers.

174 Ackermann, F., & Eden, C. (2011).

175 Ibid.

176 Hughes, R., & Beatty, K. (2005).

177 Moore & Jeon (2011).

178 Lyons, L. (2012). *Coaching at the heart of strategy* In Coaching for Leadership. (3rd ed., pp. 10-23). San Francisco, CA: Pfeiffer.

179 Kouzes, J. & Posner, B. (2012). *The leadership challenge: How to make extraordinary things happen in organizations.5th Edition*. San Francisco: CA: Joseey-Bass.

180 Winseman, A., Clifton, D., & Lieveld, C., (2008).

181 Rath, T. (2008). *Strengths based leadership: Great leaders, teams, and why people follow*. New York: NY, Gallup Press.

182 The Gallup® Organization Strengths Dashboard [About StrengthsFinder 2.0.] Retrieved from http://strengths.gallup.com/110440/About-StrengthsFinder-2.aspx.

183 Ibid.

184 Nielsen, R. (2016).

185 Sorenson, K. & Crabtree, S. (2001). *Building a team with talent*. [Gallup Business Journal]. Retrieved from

http://www.gallup.com/businessjournal/385/building-team-talent.aspx

186 Winseman, A., Clifton, D., & Lieveld, C., (2008). *Living your strengths*. (3rd ed). New York, NY: Gallup Press. 12.

187 Brutus, S. & Donia, M.A., (2010). Improving the effectiveness of students in groups with a centralized evaluation. *Academy of Management Learning & Education*, 2010, Vol. 9, No. 4, 652–662

188 Ibid.

189 Ibid.